EASY
RUSSIAN
PHRASE
BOOK

NEW EDITION

Over 700 Phrases
for Everyday Use

Sergey Levchin

D1023454

DOVER PUBLICATIONS, INC.
Mineola, New York

Bibliographical Note

Easy Russian Phrase Book NEW EDITION: Over 700 Phrases for Everyday Use
is a new work, first published by Dover Publications, Inc., in 2013.

International Standard Book Number

ISBN-13: 978-0-486-49903-1
ISBN-10: 0-486-49903-0

Manufactured in the United States by LSC Communications
49903004   2017
www.doverpublications.com

Table of Contents

Acknowledgments

I would like to thank Dover Publications for the opportunity to create this work; my editors Rochelle Kronzek and Janet Kopito for their trust and counsel; my former teachers and students at Columbia for revealing to me some of the finer mysteries of my mother tongue; and Renata Batista-Brito and Daniel Kirkeby, in whose house much of this book was drafted, and whose innocent tongues were its original proving ground.

Introduction

Using This Book

This book is designed for an English-speaking traveler with little to no previous acquaintance with the Russian language, and anticipates a traveler's basic needs and typical interactions.

Today, many of the people providing services to foreign travelers in Russia's major cities—hotel clerks, shopkeepers, waiters, bank tellers, etc.—will possess some command of English. At the same time, there will be many occasions and encounters, especially for those who would step slightly off the beaten path, where Russian will be the only means of communication.

At such times this book will help you get your point across and receive information or a service quickly, efficiently and with minimal effort.

The phrases that make up this book are largely short, straightforward and intuitive for an English-speaker, with a simple, easily graspable structure. You will understand what each word in a phrase means and how it works, and you will be able to remember the phrase better, for future use.

Naturally, the book covers all the basic constructions that a traveler may require in a variety of typical situations: *I am looking for... I need... Where is... Do you have... How can I..., etc.* Moreover, in many cases possible alternate endings, specific to the context, are offered alongside a complete phrase, for example:

Where is... a bank around here?   Где здесь... банк?
Gdye zdyes'... bank?

an ATM   банкомáт   ***ban-ka-mat***

a currency exchange   обмéн валю́ты   ***ab-myen va-lyu-tî***

In such cases, the ellipsis (...) marks the point in the sentence where a word or phrase may be replaced with an alternate word or phrase, supplied directly below.

Although this book is composed primarily of phrases that you may need to say at one time or another, these are occasionally paired with phrases that you may expect to hear and respond to. These typically appear side-by-side on the page, for example:

Your documents, please.
Ваши документы, пожалуйста.
Va-shî da-ku-myen-tî pa-zha-lus-ta.

Here are my passport and license.

Вот мой паспорт и права.

Vot moy <u>pas</u>-port i pra-<u>va</u>.

In composing each section I have tried to imagine a typical situation and follow its natural progress and possible ramifications. For example, in the *Internet* section, you will be guided through locating an Internet café or public network, asking an attendant for access information, inquiring about specific applications (for example, Skype) and hardware (printer, headphones), complaining about slow service, etc.

It is my hope that in every case you will be sufficiently "covered" by the phrases that appear in the appropriate section. At the same time, our book can hardly account for every possible instance of every encounter. Basic constructions and vocabulary, set out in the first section of this book and at the start of each section, should help you fill in many of the gaps not covered expressly.

It is, therefore, advisable to peruse the book and note down vocabulary and constructions you might consider essential, before setting out on your trip.

It is certainly possible, however, to use the book "on the fly": in this case a detailed *Index* at the back of the book will quickly guide you to the right phrase.

Pronunciation Guide

While the Russian alphabet—known as "Cyrillic"—may appear thoroughly foreign and intimidating to an English speaker, reading and pronouncing Russian is actually surprisingly easy once you have mastered the alphabet. Unlike English, where a single letter may take on a variety of different sounds, Russian letters are fairly consistent with respect to the sounds they represent. Moreover, many of these sounds are the same or very similar to those we use in English, as you can see in the table below.

Russian letter			Transliteration[1]	As in…
А	а	*а*	A a	*father, drama*
Б	б	*б*	B b	
В	в	*в*	V v	
Г	г	*г*	G g	*go, never gel*
Д	д	*д*	D d	
Е	е	*е*	E e / Ye ye	*check / yet*
Ё	ё	*ё*	Yo yo	*yogurt*
Ж	ж	*ж*	Zh zh	*measure*
З	з	*з*	Z z	
И	и	*и*	I i	*meet, ski*
Й	й	*й*	Y y	*boy*
К	к	*к*	K k	
Л	л	*л*	L l	
М	м	*м*	M m	
Н	н	*н*	N n	
О	о	*о*	O o	*more, never go or got*
П	п	*п*	P p	
Р	р	*р*	R r	
С	с	*с*	S s	
Т	т	*т*	T t	
У	у	*у*	U u	*boot*
Ф	ф	*ф*	F f	
Х	х	*х*	H h	*never silent!*
Ц	ц	*ц*	Ts ts	*lets*
Ч	ч	*ч*	Ch ch	*child*
Ш	ш	*ш*	Sh sh	*shut*
Щ	щ	*щ*	Sch sch	*sheer*
	ъ	*ъ*	' (silent)	
	ы	*ы*	î	*silly*
	ь	*ь*	' (silent)	
Э	э	*э*	E e	*met*
Ю	ю	*ю*	yu	*yule*
Я	я	*я*	ya	*yard*

Memorizing the Cyrillic alphabet and its corresponding sounds is not only useful for the purposes of this book: it will be indispensable for navigating the streets, shops, menus, etc.—as soon as you land in Russia. With a little practice you will be able to read Russian signs and inscriptions—and the phrases in this book—in their native alphabet.

If you simply pronounce Russian words as they are written, you will come very close to the correct pronunciation.

At the same time, there are certain finer points of pronunciation, not reflected in the writing, which can further facilitate your communication. To this end, every phrase in this book is supplied with an English transliteration, which will correct most of the differences between how something is written and how it is pronounced. It is, therefore, important to familiarize yourself thoroughly with the transliteration scheme given in the table above.

Here are a few examples to show you how transliteration works and to clear up any potential confusion:

Does anybody here speak English?

Кто́-нибудь здесь говори́т по-англи́йски?

Kto*-*ni*-*but' zdyes' ga*-*va*-*rit pa*-*an*-*gli*-*ski?

To make scanning the words easier I have broken them down into syllables. Stressed syllables are underlined in the transliteration (notice that accent marks appear over corresponding Russian vowels).

It is important to remember that the letters used in our transliterations **always stand for the same sound**. You may be tempted early on to read the -*but'* of *Kto*-*ni*-*but'* or the -*rit* of *ga*-*va*-*rit* as you would read them in English. Keep in mind that these vowels never change their sound, regardless of their context: our *but* sounds like *boot*, while the /i/ of -*rit* and *gli*- in the above example sound exactly alike—as the English /ee/.

Stress and Vowel Reduction

When using this book, you will probably notice that the transliteration often indicates an /a/, whereas the Russian seems to have an /o/—as in *ga*-*va*-*rit* vs. the Russian говори́т. This difference is linked directly to the stress of the word.

Certain Russian vowels change their sounds when they are not stressed—this is called "vowel reduction." A similar change occurs in English: consider the words "démocrat" and "demócracy." The sounds of the first vowel /e/ and the third vowel /a/ are "reduced" when they are unstressed—*demócracy* sounds almost like *dimócricy*. The same is true of the second vowel /o/—*démocrat* could almost be *démicrat*.

In Russian, the unstressed *o* sounds closer to an *a*—this is why in transliteration it is represented by an /a/.

Unstressed *ye* and *ya* tend to sound more like *i*—compare:

train	trip
поезд	поездка
po-ist	**pa-yest-ka**

As always, there are exceptions to the rule, but in every case the transliteration will try to get you to sound as close to correct pronunciation as possible.

Devoiced Consonants

The examples above reflect another important difference between how a word is spelled and how it is pronounced. Notice that the Russian /д/ is consistently represented by a /t/ in the transliteration.

A group of consonants—called "voiced consonants"—are changed into their "devoiced" counterparts when they occur at the end of the word (as in *поезд*), or directly before another devoiced consonant (as in *поездка*). Here are the consonant pairs in Russian and in transliteration:

voiced	devoiced	voiced	devoiced
б	п	b	p
в	ф	v	f
г	к	g	k
д	т	d	t
ж	ш	zh	sh
з	с	z	s

The voiced consonant and its devoiced pair make essentially the same sound, with the exception that the vocal chords are engaged when pronouncing the former and not engaged for the latter: try whispering the voiced consonants, and you will find that they have turned into their devoiced counterparts.

At the end of the word, voiced consonants are always "devoiced"—think *Smirnoff* (spelled *Смирнов* in Russian).

Whenever voiced and devoiced consonants "meet," the second of the two changes the sound of the first. A voiced consonant is devoiced—as in the example above: *pa-yest-ka*; and a devoiced consonant is voiced: футбол becomes *fud-bol*.

Soft Consonants

Most Russian consonants can be "hard" or "soft." When a Russian consonant is hard, it sounds more or less like its English counterpart. When it is soft—things get a little tricky.

The difference between hard and soft is similar to the difference in the *k* sound in *kill* vs. *keel*. But this difference is more pronounced in Russian and far more pervasive, affecting many more consonants.

One strategy for turning a consonant "soft" is to shape the mouth as though making a *y* sound—as in *yes*—and then pronounce the consonant.

This is the reason you will see so many *y*'s in the transliteration. For example: the consonant *д* in the word *где* is soft: if you pronounce the word as *gdye* it will sound similar to its true sound in Russian.

The vowels *е, ё, ю, я* indicate that the preceding consonant is soft—this is why we transliterate them as *ye, yo, yu, ya*: the addition of /y/ will "soften" the preceding consonants. Otherwise, these vowels are no different from their "hard" counterparts: *э, о, у, а* (transliterated: *e, o, u, a*).

The soft sign *ь* also indicates that the preceding consonant is soft—in the transliteration it is signaled by the ' . In the example given above: *kto-ni-but'*—the final /t/ is soft: *but^y*

A hard sign *ъ* signals that the preceding consonant is hard, where you would expect it to be soft—it is very rare.

The Russian r

The Russian *r* is "flapped." One trick for producing this sound that I have come across is to pronounce the phrase "Prince of Prussia" as *Puh-dince of Puh-dussia*. The tongue makes a "flap" on the *d* sound in both words—and it comes very close to the Russian *r*.

It may take some practice to nail down this "flap." If you find it too cumbersome, do not fret—pronouncing the *r* in the English fashion will still make you understood in nearly every case.

The Russian h

The Russian *h* is more aspirated—or more "breathy"—than its English counterpart, coming close to the German *achtung*! More importantly, it is never silent, as in *hour*, *honor*, *heir*, etc.

The ы Sound

This sound is not very different from the English "short" *i*—as in *it, sit, bit, kit*, etc., except a little "fuller": *silly* gets it almost perfectly (because your jaw moves forward a little in anticipation of the *l*).

Since it must be distinguished from the "long" *e* (i.e. /ee/), it is transliterated as *î*. Once more, although in English the letter /i/ changes its sound depending on its context (*bit, bite, bier*), in the transliteration /i/ will always sound like *see* and /î/ will always sound like *silly*.

Intonation

Intonation is difficult to describe on paper, and in most cases makes little difference to comprehension. In one point, however, it can make all the difference.

In Russian it is possible to change a statement into a question simply by changing the intonation:

This is a restaurant.	Is this a restaurant?
Это ресторан.	Это ресторан?
E-ta ris-ta-ran.	*E-ta ris-ta-ran?*

When making a statement, your voice will drop on the accented syllable of whatever word you are asserting: *This (place) is a restaurant*; when asking a question your voice will rise on the accented syllable of whatever word you are questioning: *Is this (place) a restaurant?*

You will probably observe that in informal English it is also possible to turn a statement into a question simply by changing the intonation. But keep in mind this important difference: in English the question *This is a restaurant?* is usually not the same as *Is this a restaurant?* In the former case you are expressing incredulity: *This (filthy dive) is a restaurant?* In Russian, however, a rising intonation is the standard and **only** way of signaling a question: thus in our case *E-ta ris-ta-ran?* is equivalent to the far more neutral question: *Is this a restaurant?*

A Note on Grammar

Russian nouns are distinguished by their **gender**: they may be masculine, feminine or neuter. Although there are some exceptions to the rule, nouns ending in consonants are typically masculine, those ending in vowels *a / ya* and the *soft sign* are typically feminine, those ending in vowels *o / ye / yo* are neuter. Endings in *i* / *î* usually signal a plural form (e.g., consider *he* / *she* / *it* / *they*: *on* / *a-<u>na</u>* / *a-<u>no</u>* / *a-<u>ni</u>*).

Russian adjectives and past tenses of verbs must agree with their nouns in **gender** and **number** (i.e., singular vs. plural). For this reason, throughout this book, you will occasionally see alternative endings given for adjectives — e.g., *kras-niy* (*na-ia*) [red] — or alternative forms given for verbs — e.g., *ya pa-<u>shol</u>/ pash-<u>la</u> (m./f.)* / *mî pash-<u>li</u> (pl.)* [I'm going, we're going].

Wherever an alternative ending is thought to be useful the masculine form will be given in full, followed by *feminine, neuter, plural* endings in parentheses: *kras-niy* (*na-ia, na-ye, nî-ye*).

Additionally, the Russian language has a **case system**: nouns and corresponding adjectives have different endings that signal their specific function in the sentence (e.g. whether the particular noun is *doing the action* or has the action *done to it*). Throughout the book you will see the same words take on different endings depending on the particular function they are serving in each situation. For example:

One ticket, please.	There are no tickets (left).
Один билет, пожалуйста.	Билетов нет.
A-din bi-lyet, pa-zha-lus-ta.	***Bi-lyet-af nyet.***

Naturally, every time a word occurs in a phrase it has been placed for you in its proper case, i.e., given a proper ending. This book does, however, include vocabulary lists, which only give the basic (nominative) form of the word.

Be assured that you will not be judged too harshly if you venture to use one of these words in a sentence, without giving it its proper case ending.

Formal Address and Politeness

In English you might address a close friend, a stranger, a superior and even a group of people with the same pronoun—*You*. This is not the case in Russian, where the informal ты (*tî*) is reserved strictly for family, friends, close acquaintances and children, while everyone else must be addressed with the polite form вы (*vî*).

Since most of your interactions in Russia will be with strangers, the phrases in this book tend to favor the polite address.

Please keep in mind that addressing a stranger—or even a recent acquaintance—with *tî* will be taken as a sign of rudeness or a deliberate slight. This is, of course, not the case among young people, where informal language is the norm. At the same time, it would be highly unwise to address your waiter, hotel clerk or anyone else in the service industry—however young—with the informal *tî*.

The phrases in this book may seem to you overly polite, with *please* (*pa-zha-lus-ta*), accompanying nearly every request. In English we often "soften" our requests through a variety of strategies, for example: *Could you help me with this? Would you mind helping me with this?* Although Russian is also capable of such indirect language, the standard means of making a polite request is to use *please*, as in: *Please help me with this.*

It would be very difficult to use "Please" *too* frequently; therefore, do not drop it from phrases, even if you might think it superfluous or redundant.

Chapter 1
Basic Conversation

BASIC NECESSITIES

1. Yes. Да. ***Da.***

2. No. Нет. ***Nyet.***

3. Thank you. Спасибо. ***Spa-<u>si</u>-ba.***

4. Please *and* You're welcome. Пожалуйста.
Pa-<u>zha</u>-lus-ta.

5. Ok. Fine. Хорошо. ***Ha-ra-<u>sho</u>.***

6. Excuse me. Извините. ***Iz-vi-<u>ni</u>-tye.***

7. It's nothing. Ничего. ***Ni-chi-<u>vo</u>.***

8. Help! Помогите! ***Pa-ma-<u>gi</u>-tye!***

9. Everything is okay. Всё в порядке. ***Vsyo fpa-<u>ryat</u>-kye.***

10. May I? Можно? ***<u>Mozh</u>-na?***

11. No need. Не нужно. ***Ni-<u>nuzh</u>-na.***

12. Where is the bathroom? Где туалет? ***Gdye tu-a-<u>lyet</u>?***

13. How much? Сколько? ***<u>Skol'</u>-ka?***

14. Show me. Покажите. ***Pa-ka-<u>zhi</u>-tye.***

15. Where is…? Где…? ***Gdye…?***

16. Here is…   Вот…   *Vot…*

COMPREHENSION

17. What?   Что?   *Shto?*

18. What did you say?   Что вы сказáли?   *Shto vî ska-za-li?*

19. I don't speak Russian.   Я не говорю́ по-рýсски.
     Ya ni-ga-va-ryu pa-rus-ki.

20. Do you speak English?   Вы говори́те по-англи́йски?
     Vî ga-va-ri-tye pa-an-gli-ski?

21. I speak Russian badly.   Я плóхо говорю́ по-рýсски.
     Ya plo-ha ga-va-ryu pa-rus-ki.

22. I speak… English.   Я говорю́… по-англи́йски.
     Ya ga-va-ryu… pa-an-gli-ski.

     German.   по-немéцки.   *pa-ni-myets-ki.*

     Spanish.   по-испáнски.   *pa-is-pan-ski.*

     French.   по-францýзски.   *pa-fran-tsu-ski.*

23. Do you understand?   Вы понимáете?
     Vî pa-ni-may-tye?

24. I (don't) understand.   Я (не) понимáю.
     Ya (ni-) pa-ni-ma-yu.

25. Repeat, please.   Повтори́те, пожáлуйста.
     Paf-ta-ri-tye pa-zha-lus-ta.

26. Slowly, please.   Мéдленнее, пожáлуйста.
     Myed-li-ni-ye, pa-zha-lus-ta.

27. What does this mean?   Что э́то знáчит?
     Shto e-ta zna-chit?

28. What does [Russian word] mean?   Что знáчит… ?
     Shto zna-chit… ?

29. How do you say [English word] in Russian?
     Как по-рýсски… ?
     Kak pa-rus-ki… ?

30. Does anybody here speak English?
    Кто́-нибудь здесь говори́т по-англи́йски?
    Kto-ni-but' zdyes' ga-va-_rit_ pa-an-_gli_-ski?

31. Please speak Russian.   Говори́те по-ру́сски, пожа́луйста.
    Ga-va-_ri_-tye pa-_rus_-ki pa-_zha_-lus-ta.

GREETINGS AND INTRODUCTIONS

32. Hello.   Здра́вствуйте.   **_Zdra_-stvuy-tye.**

33. Good-bye.   До свида́ния.   **Da-svi-_da_-nya.**

34. Hi.   Приве́т.   **Pri-_vyet_.**

35. Bye.   Пока́.   **Pa-_ka_.**

36. Good afternoon.   До́брый день.   **_Do_-briy dyen'.**

37. Good morning.   До́брое у́тро.   **_Do_-bra-ye _u_-tra.**

38. Good evening.   До́брый ве́чер.   **_Do_-briy _vye_-chir.**

39. How's it going?   Как дела́?   **Kak di-_la_?**

40. Everything's... fine.   Всё... хорошо́.   **Fsyo... ha-ra-_sho_.**
    great!   отли́чно!   **at-_lich_-na!**
    okay.   норма́льно.   **nar-_mal'_-na.**

41. What is your name?   Как вас зову́т?   **Kak vas za-_vut_?**

42. My name is...   Меня́ зову́т...   **Mi-nya za-_vut_...**

43. Who is that?   Кто́ это?   **_Kto_-e-ta?**

44. This is my... friend.   Э́то мой... друг.
    _E_-ta moy... druk.
    husband.   муж.   **mush.**
    brother.   брат.   **brat.**
    father.   оте́ц.   **a-_tyets_.**
    son.   сын.   **sîn.**
    partner.   партнёр.   **part-_nyor_.**

45. This is my… girlfriend.   Э́то моя́… подру́га.
    E-ta ma-ya… pa-dru-ga.
    wife.   жена́.   *zhî-na.*
    sister.   сестра́.   *si-stra.*
    mother.   мать.   *mat'.*
    daughter.   дочь.   *doch'.*
    family.   семья́.   *si-mya.*

46. This is… John.   Э́то… Джон.   *E-ta… Dzhon.*
    Mary.   Мэ́ри.   *Me-ri.*
    Mr. Ivanov.   господи́н Ивано́в.   *gas-pa-din I-va-nof*
    Ms. Smith.   госпожа́ Смит.   *gas-pa-zha Smit.*

47. Have you met?   Вы знако́мы?   *Vî zna-ko-mî?*

48. Do you know… my friend Maksim?
    Ты зна́ешь… моего́ дру́га Макси́ма?
    Tî zna-yish… ma-yi-vo dru-ga Mak-si-ma?
    Mr. Ivanov?   господи́на Ивано́ва?
    gas-pa-di-na I-va-no-va?

49. Yes, we've met.   Да, мы знако́мы.   *Da, mî zna-ko-mî.*

50. No, we haven't met.   Нет, мы не знако́мы.
    Nyet, mî ni-zna-ko-mî.

51. Glad to meet you.   Прия́тно познако́миться.
    Pri-yat-na pa-zna-ko-mit-sa.

52. Very nice (to meet you).   О́чень прия́тно.
    O-chin' pri-yat-na.

PERSONAL INFORMATION

53. How old are you (is she /he)?
    Ско́лько вам (ей /ему́) лет?
    Skol'-ka vam (yey /yi-mu) lyet?

54. I am thirty-seven.   Мне три́дцать семь лет.
    Mnye <u>tri</u>-tsat' syem' lyet.

55. And you?   А вам?   *A vam?*

56. Where are you from?   Отку́да вы?   *At-<u>ku</u>-da vî?*

57. Where do you live?   Где вы живёте?
    Gdye vî zhî-<u>vyo</u>-tye?

58. I am from... the U.S.   Я из... Аме́рики.
    Ya iz... A-<u>mye</u>-ri-ki.

    Canada.   Кана́ды.   *Ka-<u>na</u>-dî.*

    UK.   А́нглии.   *<u>Ang</u>-li-i.*

    Australia.   Австра́лии.   *Af-<u>stra</u>-li-i.*

59. We live in... New York.   Мы живём в... Нью-Йо́рке.
    Mî zhî-<u>vyom</u> v... Nyu-<u>yor</u>-kye.

    Chicago.   Чика́го.   *Chi-<u>ka</u>-ga.*

    Los Angeles.   Лос-А́нжелесе.   *Los-<u>an</u>-zhî-li-sye.*

60. What do you do?   Чем вы занима́етесь?
    Chem vî za-ni-<u>may</u>-tis'?

61. I am... a doctor.   Я... врач.   *Ya... vrach.*

    scientist.   учёный.   *u-<u>cho</u>-nîy.*

    journalist.   журнали́ст.   *zhur-na-<u>list</u>.*

    student.   студе́нт.   *stu-<u>dyent.</u>*

62. I don't work.   Я не рабо́таю.   *Ya ni-ra-<u>bo</u>-ta-yu.*

63. We are retired.   Мы на пе́нсии.   *Mî na <u>pyen</u>-si-i.*

64. And you?   А вы?   *A vî?*

65. I work... in a hospital.   Я рабо́таю... в больни́це.
    Ya ra-<u>bo</u>-ta-yu... v-bal'-<u>ni</u>-tse.

    at a firm.   в фи́рме.   *<u>ffir</u>-mye.*

    at a university.   в университе́те.   *vu-ni-ver-si-<u>tye</u>-tye.*

    in a bank.   в ба́нке.   *v-<u>ban</u>-kye.*

66. Where do you study?   Где вы́учитесь?
Gdye vî u-chi-tis'?

67. What do you study?   Что вы изуча́ете?
Shto vî i-zu-chay-tye?

68. I study at Columbia University in New York.
Я учу́сь в Колумби́йском университе́те в Нью-Йо́рке.
*Ya u-chus' fKa-lum-biy-skam u-ni-vyer-si-tye-tye
vNyu-yor-kye.*

69. I am studying to be… a doctor.   Я учу́сь на… врача́.
Ya u-chus' na… vra-cha.

    programmer.   программи́ста.   *pra-gra-mis-ta.*

    engineer.   инженéра.   *in-zhi-nye-ra.*

70. I study… literature.   Я изуча́ю… литерату́ру.
Ya i-zu-cha-yu… li-te-ra-tu-ru.

    languages.   языки́.   *yi-zî-ki.*

    business.   би́знес.   *biz-nes.*

    sociology.   социоло́гию.   *sa-tsî-a-lo-gi-yu.*

71. Are you married? (m.)   Вы жена́ты?   *Vî zhi-na-tî?*

    Are you married? (f.)   Вы за́мужем?   *Vî za-mu-zhîm?*

72. Do you have children?   У вас есть де́ти?
U vas yest' dye-ti?

73. I am (not) married. (m.)   Я (не) жена́т.
Ya (ni-) zhî-nat.

    I am (not) married. (f.)   Я (не) за́мужем.
Ya (ni-) za-mu-zhîm.

74. I am divorced.   Я в разво́де.   *Ya vraz-vo-dye.*

75. I live with a partner.   Я живу́ с партнёром.
Ya zhî-vu spart-nyo-ram.

76. We have… no children. У нас… нет детей.
    U nas… nyet di-<u>tey</u>.

    two. двóе. *<u>dvo</u>-ye.*

    three. трóе. *<u>tro</u>-ye.*

77. I have a… son. У меня́… сын. *U mi-<u>nya</u>… sîn.*

    daughter. дочь. *doch'.*

78. Where are your children? Где вáши дéти?
    Gdye <u>va</u>-shî <u>dye</u>-ti?

79. They are (not) with us. Они́ (не) с нáми.
    A-<u>ni</u> (ni-) <u>sna</u>-mi.

80. Are you a tourist / tourists? Вы тури́ст / тури́сты?
    Vî tu-<u>rist</u> / tu-<u>ris</u>-tî.

81. I am (not) a tourist. Я (не) тури́ст. *Ya (nye) tu-<u>rist</u>.*

82. I am here for work. Я здесь по рабóте.
    Ya zdyes' pa-ra-<u>bo</u>-tye.

83. We are on vacation. Мы в óтпуске. *Mî <u>vot</u>-pus-kye.*

84. I'm on break. Я на кани́кулах. *Ya na-ka-<u>ni</u>-ku-lah.*

TIME AND DATE

85. What time is it? Котóрый час? *Ka-<u>to</u>-rîy chas?*

86. One pm / am. Час дня / нóчи. *Chas dnya / <u>no</u>-chi.*

87. Five in the morning / evening. Пять утрá / вéчера.
    Pyat' u-<u>tra</u> / <u>vye</u>-chi-ra.

88. Noon. Пóлдень. *<u>Pol</u>-din'.*

89. Midnight. Пóлночь. *<u>Pol</u>-nach'.*

90. Two-oh-five (2:05). Два ноль пять. *Dva nol' pyat'.*

91. One-twenty (1:20). Час двáдцать. *Chas <u>dva</u>-tsat'.*

92. Quarter past twelve.   Чётверть пе́рвого.
     Chyet-virt' pyer-va-va.

93. Quarter to eleven.   Без че́тверти оди́ннадцать.
     Bis-chyet-vir-ti a-di-na-tsat'.

94. Half past.   Полови́на.   *Pa-la-vi-na.*

95. What day is it today?   Како́й сего́дня день?
     Ka-koy si-vod-nya dyen'?

96. Today is Monday.   Сего́дня понеде́льник.
     Si-vod-nya pa-ni-dyel'-nik.

97. Yesterday was Sunday.   Вчера́ бы́ло воскресе́нье.
     Fchi-ra bî-la vas-kri-syen-ye.

98. Tomorrow is Tuesday.   За́втра бу́дет вто́рник.
     Zaf-tra bu-dit ftor-nik.

99. What is the date today?   Како́е сего́дня число́?
     Ka-ko-ye si-vod-nya chis-lo?

100. The twenty-third of February.   Два́дцать тре́тье февраля́.
     Dva-tsat' trye-tye fiv-ra-lya.

Chapter 2
Getting Around

DIRECTIONS

101. Excuse me, I am looking for Revolution Square.
Извини́те, я ищу́ Пло́щадь Револю́ции.
Iz-vi-ni-tye, ya i-schu Plo-schit' Ri-va-lyu-tsî-i.

102. Where is... the Hermitage located?
Где нахо́дится... Эрмита́ж?
Gdye na-ho-dit-sa... Er-mi-tash?

Rizhskii market.   Ри́жский ры́нок.   *Rish-skiy rî-nak.*

Khlebnyi Lane.   Хле́бный переу́лок.
Hlyeb-nîy pi-ri-u-lak.

103. Where is there a metro station around here?
Где здесь... ста́нция метро́?
Gdye szdyes'... stan-tsî-ya mit-ro?

104. Where is there a restaurant around here?
Где здесь... рестора́н.
Gdye szdyes'... ris-ta-ran.

bathroom.   туале́т.   *tu-a-lyet*

105. It's over there.   Э́то вон там.   *E-ta von tam.*

106. I (don't) see it.   Я (не) ви́жу.   *Ya (ni-) vi-zhu.*

107. Is it far?   Э́то далеко́?   *E-ta da-li-ko?*

108. It's (not) far from here.   Э́то (не)далеко́ отсю́да.
E-ta (ni-) da-li-ko at-syu-da.

109. It's… on Prechistenka St.　　Это… на Пречистéнке.
E-ta… na-Pri-chis-tyen-ke.

near the Lubianka station.　　рядом со стáнцией Лубянка.
rya-dam sa-stan-tsî-yey Lu-byan-ka.

across the street.　　через дорóгу.　　*chi-ris-da-ro-gu.*

at the corner.　　на углý.　　*na-ug-lu.*

around the corner.　　за углóм.　　*za-ug-lom.*

downtown.　　в цéнтре гóрода.　　*ftsent-rye go-ra-da.*

out of town.　　за гóродом.　　*za-go-ra-dam.*

110. Could you please tell me how to get to… downtown?
Скажите, пожáлуйста, как добрáться до… цéнтра?
Ska-zhî-tye, pa-zha-lus-ta, kak da-brat'-sya da… tsen-tra?

the airport.　　аэропóрта.　　*a-e-ra-por-ta.*

the Sokol metro station.　　стáнции метрó Сóкол.
stan-tsî-i mi-tro So-kal.

Tverskaia St.　　Тверскóй.　　*Tvir-skoy.*

111. Go straight.　　Идите прямо.　　*I-di-tye prya-ma.*

112. Turn right / left.　　Поверните напрáво / налéво.
Pa-vir-ni-tye na-pra-va / na-lye-va.

113. Turn around.　　Развернитесь.　　*Raz-vir-ni-tyes'.*

114. Walk two blocks.　　Пройдите два квартáла.
Pray-di-tye dva kvar-ta-la.

115. Turn onto Arbat Street.　　Поверните на Арбáт.
Pa-vir-ni-tye na-Ar-bat.

116. Is it a long walk / ride?　　Тудá дóлго идти / éхать?
Tu-da dol-ga i-ti / ye-hat'?

117. About fifteen minutes.　　Минýт пятнáдцать.
Mi-nut pit-na-tsat'.

USING A MAP

118. Do you have a map of the city?   У вас есть ка́рта го́рода?
   U-vas yest' kar-ta go-ra-da?

119. Where can I buy a map of the city?
   Где мо́жно купи́ть ка́рту го́рода?
   Gdye mozh-na ku-pit' kar-tu go-ra-da?

120. Please, show me on the map.
   Покажи́те, пожа́луйста, на ка́рте.
   Pa-ka-zhî-tye, pa-zha-lus-ta, na-kar-tye.

121. What street is this?   Кака́я э́то у́лица?
   Ka-ka-ya e-ta u-li-tsa?

122. Where are we now?   Где мы сейча́с?
   Gdye mî siy-chas?

123. We are here.   Мы здесь.   *Mî zdyes'.*

124. I need to get over there.   Мне ну́жно попа́сть сюда́.
   Mnye nuzh-na pa-past' syu-da.

LOCATING AN ADDRESS

125. What address are you looking for?
   Како́й а́дрес вам ну́жен?
   Ka-koy ad-ris vam nu-zhîn?

126. Nikolskaia Street, number 15, apartment 2.
   У́лица Нико́льская, дом пятна́дцать, кварти́ра два.
   U-li-tsa Ni-kol'-ska-ya, dom pit-na-tsat', kvar-ti-ra dva.

127. What is your address?   Како́й у вас а́дрес?
   Ka-koy u-vas ad-ris?

128. My address is…   Мой а́дрес…   *Moy ad-ris…*

129. I'm looking for the address…   Я ищу́ а́дрес…
   Ya i-schu ad-ris…

130. What is the... house number here?
Какóй здесь... нóмер дóма?
Ka-koy zdyes'... no-mir do-ma?

apartment number.   нóмер квартúры.
no-mir kvar-ti-rî.

131. What is the address of... your hotel?
Какóй áдрес у... вáшей гостúницы?
Ka-koy ad-ris u... va-shîy gas-ti-ni-tsî?

your office.   вáшего óфиса.   *va-shî-va o-fi-sa.*

the movie theater.   кинотеáтра.   *ki-na-ti-at-ra.*

METRO

132. One ride, please.   Однá поéздка, пожáлуйста.
Ad-na pa-yest-ka, pa-zha-lus-ta.

Two rides.   Две поéздки.   *Dvye pa-yest-ki*

Ten rides.   Дéсять поéздок.   *Dye-sit' pa-yez-dak.*

133. A monthly pass, please.
Проезднóй на мéсяц, пожáлуйста.
Pra-yizd-noy na-mye-sits, pa-zha-lus-ta.

134. A 30-day smart card.   Смáрт-кáрту на трúдцать дней.
Smart-kar-tu na-tri-tsat' dnyey.

135. Where can I buy / charge a smart card?
Где мóжно купúть / зарядúть смáрт-кáрту?
Gdye mozh-na ku-pit' / za-rya-dit' smart-kar-tu?

136. What station / line is this?   Какáя э́то стáнция / лúния?
Ka-ka-ya e-ta stan-tsî-ya / li-ni-ya?

137. What is the next station?   Какáя слéдующая стáнция?
Ka-ka-ya slye-duy-scha-ya stan-tsî-ya?

138. How can I get to Taganskaia station?
Как мне попáсть на стáнцию Тагáнская?
Kak mnye pa-past' na-stan-tsî-yu Ta-gan-ska-ya?

139. Does this train go to Park Pobedy?
Этот поезд идёт до станции Парк Победы?
E-tat po-yist i-dyot da-stan-tsî-i Park Pa-bye-dî?

140. Where is the walkway to Pushkinskaia station?
Где переход на станцию Пушкинская?
Gdye pi-ri-hod na-stan-tsî-yu Push-kin-ska-ya?

141. It's up the… stairs.   Это вверх по… лестнице.
E-ta vvyerh pa… lyes-ni-tse.

escalator.   эскалатору.   *es-ka-la-ta-ru.*

142. Could you please tell me where I can transfer to the Circle Line?
Скажите, пожалуйста, где можно пересесть на кольцевую линию?
Ska-zhî-tye, pa-zha-lus-ta, gdye mozh-na pi-ri-syest' na-kal'-tsî-vu-yu li-ni-yu?

143. You need to get off at Chkalovskaia and transfer over to Kurskaia.
Вам нужно выйти на Чкаловской и пересесть на Курскую.
Vam nuzh-na vîy-ti na Chka-laf-skay i pi-ri-syest' na-Kur-sku-yu.

144. Are you getting off?   Вы выходите?   *Vî vî-ho-di-tye?*

145. I'm getting off.   Я выхожу.   *Ya vî-ha-zhu.*

146. Please let me through.   Пропустите, пожалуйста.
Pra-pus-ti-tye, pa-zha-lus-ta.

147. Attention, the doors are closing!
Осторожно, двери закрываются!
As-ta-rozh-na, dvye-ri za-krî-va-yut-sya.

BUS, TROLLEY, TRAM, SHUTTLE

148. Excuse me, is this a… bus stop?
Извините, здесь остановка… автобуса?
Iz-vi-ni-tye, zdyes' as-ta-nof-ka… af-to-bu-sa?

trolley.   троллейбуса.   *tra-ley-bu-sa.*

shuttle.   маршрутки.   *marsh-rut-ki.*

149. Which (route) number do you need?
Какой номер вам нужен?
Ka-koy no-mir vam nu-zhîn?

150. I need number 45.   Мне нужен сорок пятый.
Mnye nu-zhîn so-rak pya-tîy.

151. Do you know when the next bus is due?
Вы не знаете, когда следующий автобус?
Vî ni-znay-tye, kag-da slye-duy-schiy af-to-bus?

152. Do you have a schedule?   У вас нет расписания?
U-vas nyet ras-pi-sa-ni-ya?

153. Have you been waiting long?   Вы уже давно ждёте?
Vî u-zhe dav-no zhdyo-tye?

154. How much is a single ride?   Сколько стоит проезд?
Skol'-ka sto-it pra-yest?

155. I have no change.   У меня нет сдачи.
U-mi-nya nyet zda-chi.

156. Does this tram go to... Red Square?
Этот трамвай идёт до... Красной площади?
E-tat tram-vay i-dyot da... Kras-nay plo-schi-di?

157. What route (number) is this?   Какой это маршрут?
Ka-koy e-ta marsh-rut?

158. I need to get to Vinzavod.
Мне нужно попасть на Винзавод.
Mnye nuzh-na pa-past' na-Vin-za-vot.

159. Please let me know when to get off.
Пожалуйста, дайте знать, когда мне выходить.
Pa-zha-lust-ta, day-tye znat', kag-da mnye vî-ha-dit'.

160. Let me off here.   Выпустите меня здесь.
Vî-pus-ti-tye mi-nya zdyes'.

TAXI

161. I need a taxi.   Мне нýжно таксú.
Mnye _nuzh_-na tak-_si_.

162. At what time?   В котóром часý?   **Fka-_to_-ram cha-_su_?**

163. Tomorrow, at 8:30 a.m.   Зáвтра, в вóсемь трúдцать утрá.
Zaf-tra, v-_vo_-sim' _tri_-tsat' u-_tra_.

164. Where are you located?   Где вы нахóдитесь?
Gdye vî na-_ho_-di-tyes'?

165. Here is the address.   Вот áдрес.   **Vot _ad_-ris.**

166. Where are you going?   Кудá вы éдете?
Ku-_da_ vî _ye_-di-tye?

167. I need to get to the Kremlin.   Мне нýжно в Крéмль.
Mnye _nuzh_-na fKryeml'.

168. How much will it cost?   Скóлько э́то бýдет стóить?
Skol'-ka _e_-ta _bu_-dit _sto_-it'?

169. It's too expensive!   Э́то слúшком дóрого!
E-ta _slish_-kam _do_-ra-ga!

170. Please turn on the meter.
Пожáлуйста, включúте счётчик.
Pa-_zha_-lus-ta, fklyu-_chi_-tye _schyot_-chik.

171. Please turn off… the radio.
Пожáлуйста, вы́ключите… рáдио.
Pa-_zha_-lus-ta, _vî_-klyu-chi-tye… _ra_-di-o.

air conditioner.   кондиционéр.   **kan-di-tsî-a-_nyer_.**

172. Please open the window.   Пожáлуйста, открóйте окнó.
Pa-_zha_-lus-ta, at-_kroy_-tye ak-_no_.

173. Please go a little... faster.
Пожа́луйста чу́ть... быстре́е.
*Pa-**zha**-lus-ta chut'... bîs-**trye**-ye.*

slower.   ме́дленнее.   *__myed__-li-ni-ye.*

174. I'm running late.   Я опа́здываю.   *Ya a-__paz__-di-va-yu.*

TRAINS AND COMMUTER RAIL

175. Pardon me, where are the ticket counters?
Извини́те, где биле́тные ка́ссы?
Iz-vi-__ni__-tye, gdye bi-__lyet__-nî-ye __kas__-sî?

176. Please give me two tickets to Vorkuta.
Да́йте, пожа́луйста, два биле́та на Воркуту́.
__Dai__-tye, pa-__zha__-lus-ta, dva bi-__lye__-ta na-Var-ku-__tu__.

177. One way.   В оди́н коне́ц.   *Va-__din__ ka-__nyets__.*

178. Two beds in a sleeping compartment.   Два ме́ста в купе́.
Dva __myes__-ta fku-__pe__.

179. One coach ticket.   Оди́н плацка́ртный биле́т.
A-__din__ plats-__kart__-nîy bi-__lyet__.

180. At what time does the train depart?
В кото́ром часу́ ухо́дит по́езд?
Fka-__to__-ram cha-__su__ u-__ho__-dit __po__-yist?

181. From which platform does the St. Petersburg train depart?
С како́го пути́ ухо́дит пи́терский по́езд?
Ska-__ko__-va pu-__ti__ u-__ho__-dit pi-tir-skiy __po__-yist?

182. Where is the train for Cheboksary?
Где по́езд на Чебокса́ры?
Gdye __po__-yist na-Chi-bak-__sa__-rî?

183. Which way to the trains?   Где вы́ход к поезда́м?
Gdye __vî__-hat kpa-yiz-__dam__?

184. Where is platform number 15?
Где платфо́рма но́мер пятна́дцать?
Gdye plat-__for__-ma __no__-mir pit-__na__-tsat'?

185. Where are the sleeping cars?   Где купейные вагоны?
     Gdye ku-<u>pey</u>-ni-ye va-<u>go</u>-ni?

186. Is there a dining car on this train?
     В этом поезде есть вагон-ресторан?
     <u>Ve</u>-tam <u>po</u>-yiz-dye yest' va-<u>gon</u> ris-ta-<u>ran</u>?

187. What car number is this?   Какой это вагон?
     Ka-<u>koy</u> e-ta va-<u>gon</u>?

188. What seat number is this?   Какое это место?
     Ka-<u>ko</u>-ye e-ta <u>myes</u>-ta?

189. Excuse me, this is… my seat.   Извините, это… моё место.
     Iz-vi-<u>ni</u>-tye, e-ta… ma-<u>yo</u> <u>myes</u>-ta.

     our compartment.   наше купе.   *<u>na</u>-she ku-<u>pe</u>.*

RENTING A CAR

190. I had reserved a car under the name Hardy.
     Я бронировал машину на имя Харди.
     Ya bra-<u>ni</u>-ra-val ma-<u>shi</u>-nu na-i-mya <u>Har</u>-di.

191. I'd like to rent a car for five days.
     Я хотел бы взять машину на пять дней.
     Ya ha-<u>tyel</u>-bi vzyat' ma-<u>shi</u>-nu na-<u>pyat'</u> dnyey.

192. What kind of cars do you have?
     Какие у вас есть машины?
     Ka-<u>ki</u>-ye u-<u>vas</u> yest' ma-<u>shi</u>-ni?

193. Automatic or manual transmission?
     Автоматическая или ручная трансмиссия?
     Af-ta-ma-<u>ti</u>-chis-ka-ya <u>i</u>-li ruch-<u>na</u>-ya trans-<u>mis</u>-si-ya?

194. How much is it per day?   Сколько это стоит в день?
     <u>Skol'</u>-ka e-ta <u>sto</u>-it vdyen'?

195. I (don't) need insurance.   Мне (не) нужна страховка.
     Mnye (ni-) nuzh-<u>na</u> stra-<u>hof</u>-ka.

196. I will pay with a credit card.   Я плачу кредиткой.
     Ya pla-<u>chu</u> kri-<u>dit</u>-kay.

BUYING GASOLINE

197. Where is there a gas station around here?
Где здесь запра́вка?
Gdye zdyes' za-praf-ka?

198. Please fill up my car with 1,000 rubles' worth (of gasoline).
Пожа́луйста, запра́вьте маши́ну на ты́сячу рубле́й.
Pa-zha-lus-ta, za-praf-tye ma-shi-nu na-ti-si-chu rub-lyey.

199. Fill up the tank.   Нале́йте по́лный бак.
Na-lyey-tye pol-niy bak.

200. What type of gasoline would you like?
Како́й вам бензи́н?
Ka-koy vam bin-zin?

201. Eighty / Ninety-three.
Восьмидеся́тый / Девяно́сто тре́тий.
Vas'-mi-di-sya-tiy / Di-vi-nos-ta trye-tiy.

202. Do you have… motor oil?   У вас есть… мото́рное ма́сло?
U-vas yest'… ma-tor-na-ye mas-la?

antifreeze.   антифри́з.   ***an-ti-fris.***

brake fluid.   тормозна́я жи́дкость.
tar-maz-na-ya zhit-kast'.

203. Can you change the oil?   Вы мо́жете поменя́ть ма́сло?
Vi mo-zhi-tye pa-mi-nyat' mas-la?

204. My card is not working (at the pump).
Моя́ ка́рточка не рабо́тает (у коло́нки).
Ma-ya kar-tach-ka ni-ra-bo-ta-yit (u-ka-lon-ki).

TRAFFIC VIOLATIONS

205. Your documents, please.   Ва́ши докуме́нты, пожа́луйста.
Va-shi da-ku-myen-ti, pa-zha-lus-ta.

206. Here are my passport and driver's license.
Вот мой па́спорт и права́.
Vot moy pas-port i-pra-va.

207. This is a rental car.   Это рентóваная машúна.
E-ta rin-to-va-na-ya ma-shî-na.

208. Here are all the documents.   Вот все докумéнты.
Vot fsye da-ku-myen-tî.

209. Have you been drinking?   Вы пúли?   **Vî pyi-li?**

210. I haven't been drinking.   Я ничегó не пил.
Ya ni-chi-vo ni-pil.

211. Your... driver's license is invalid.
Вáши... правá недействúтельны.
Va-shî... pra-va ni-diy-stvi-til'-nî.

insurance.   страхóвка.   **stra-hof-ka.**

212. This is a stolen vehicle.   Эта машúна крáденая.
E-ta ma-shî-na kra-di-na-ya.

213. You were speeding.   Вы превы́сили скóрость.
Vî pri-vî-si-li sko-rast'.

214. You went through a red light.
Вы проéхали на крáсный свет.
Vî pra-ye-ha-li na-kras-nîy svyet.

215. Your headlights are out.   У вас фáры не горя́т.
U-vas fa-rî ni-ga-ryat.

216. Turn off the engine.   Вы́ключите мотóр.
U-vas-chi-tye ma-tor.

217. Step out of the vehicle.   Вы́йдите из машúны.
Vîy-di-tye iz-ma-shî-nî.

218. Follow me.   Слéдуйте за мной.
Slye-duy-tye za-mnoy.

219. How much will this cost?
Скóлько это бýдет стóить?
Skol'-ka e-ta bu-dit sto-it'?

CAR TROUBLE AND ACCIDENTS

220. Is there a service station near here?
Где́-нибудь здесь есть автосе́рвис?
Gdye-ni-but' zdyes' yest' afto-ser-vis?

221. My car has broken down.   У меня́ слома́лась маши́на.
U-mi-nya sla-ma-las' ma-shî-na.

222. I've been in an accident.   Я попа́л в ава́рию.
Ya pa-pal va-va-ri-yu.

223. I got a flat tire.   Я проколо́л ши́ну.
Ya pra-ka-lol shî-nu.

224. The battery is dead.   Аккумуля́тор сел.
A-ku-mu-lya-tar syel.

225. Could you give me a "jump"?   Помоги́те мне завести́сь?
Pa-ma-gi-tye mnye za-vis-tis'?

226. I don't have jumper cables.   У меня́ нет ка́беля.
U-mi-nya nyet ka-bi-lya.

227. The car… won't go.   Маши́на… не е́дет.
Ma-shî-na… ni-ye-dit.

isn't starting.   не заво́дится.   *ni-za-vo-dit-sa.*

is overheating.   перегрева́ется.   *pi-ri-gri-va-yit-sa.*

is smoking.   дыми́тся.   *di-mit-sa.*

228. The car is stuck.   Маши́на застря́ла.
Ma-shî-na za-strya-la.

229. I'm out of gas.   Ко́нчился бензи́н.
Kon-chil-sya bin-zin.

230. I've locked the keys inside.   Я за́пер ключи́ внутри́.
Ya za-pir klyu-chi vnu-tri.

231. Please help me push the car.
Помоги́те подтолкну́ть маши́ну.
Pa-ma-gi-tye pat-talk-nut' ma-shî-nu.

232. Please tow the car to the nearest service station.
Пожалуйста, оттащите машину на близжайший сервис.
Pa-zha-lus-ta, at-ta-schi-tye ma-shî-nu na-bli-zhay-shîy
ser-vis.

AIR TRAVEL

233. I would like to reserve a ticket to Magadan.
Я хочу забронировать билет в Магадан.
Ya ha-chu za-bra-ni-ra-vat' bi-lyet vMa-ga-dan.

234. I need to check in (for boarding).
Мне нужно зарегистрироваться (на посадку).
Mnye nuzh-na za-ri-gist-ri-ra-vat-sa (na-pa-sat-ku).

235. I have an electronic ticket.   У меня электронный билет.
U-mi-nya e-lik-tron-nîy bi-lyet.

236. I've already checked in online.
Я уже зарегистрировался по интернету.
Ya u-zhe za-ri-gist-ri-ra-val-sa pa-In-ter-ne-tu.

237. Where are you flying to?   Куда вы летите?
Ku-da vî li-ti-tye?

238. I'm flying to Krasnodar.   Я лечу в Краснодар.
Ya li-chu fKras-na-dar.

239. What airline?   Какая авиалиния?
Ka-ka-ya a-vi-a-li-ni-ya?

240. What is the flight number?   Какой номер рейса?
Ka-koy no-mir rey-sa?

241. What terminal is this?   Какой это терминал?
Ka-koy e-ta ter-mi-nal?

242. How can I get to Terminal A?
Как попасть на терминал А?
Kak pa-past' na-ter-mi-nal A?

243. I need to check my luggage.   Мне нужно сдать багаж.
Mnye nuzh-na zdat' ba-gash.

244. One suitcase.   Оди́н чемода́н.   **A-_din_ chi-ma-_dan_.**

245. This is a carry-on.   Это ручна́я кладь.
E-ta ruch-_na_-ya klat'.

246. Do we have to go through customs?
Нам ну́жно пройти́ тамо́жню?
Nam _nuzh_-na pray-_ti_ ta-_mozh_-nyu?

247. You need to go through security.
Вам ну́жно пройти́ досмо́тр.
Vam _nuzh_-na pray-_ti_ da-_smotr_.

248. Is this your bag?   Это ва́ша су́мка?
E-ta _va_-sha _sum_-ka?

249. What is in your bag?   Что у вас в су́мке?
Shto u-_vas_ _fsum_-kye?

250. What time is boarding?   Когда́ поса́дка?
Kag-_da_ pa-_sat_-ka?

251. Boarding is delayed.   Поса́дка заде́рживается.
Pa-_sat_-ka za-_dyer_-zhî-va-yit-sa.

252. The flight is canceled.   Рейс отменён.
Ryeys at-mi-_nyon_.

253. Where is the baggage claim?   Где вы́дача багажа́?
Gdye _vî_-da-cha ba-ga-_zha_?

254. I can't find… my luggage.   Я не могу́ найти́… свой бага́ж.
Ya ni-ma-_gu_ nay-_ti_… svoy ba-_gash_.

    my bag.   свою́ су́мку.   **sva-_yu_ _sum_-ku.**

    my backpack.   свой рюкза́к.   **svoy ryug-_zak_.**

255. This is (not) my suitcase.   Это (не) мой чемода́н.
_E_-ta (ni-) moy chi-ma-_dan_.

CROSSING BORDERS

256. Your first name, last name, patronymic.
Ваше имя, фамилия, отчество.
Va-she i-mya, fa-mi-li-ya, ot-chist-va.

257. Your passport, please.   Ваш паспорт, пожалуйста.
Vash pas-port, pa-zha-lus-ta.

258. Here is... my passport.   Вот... мой паспорт.
Vot... moy pas-port.

my visa.   моя виза.   *ma-ya vi-za.*

my migration card.   моя миграционная карточка.
ma-ya mi-gra-tsî-on-na-ya kar-tach-ka.

259. I don't have... a visa.   У меня нет... визы.
U-mi-nya nyet... vi-zî.

migration card.   миграционной карточки.
mi-gra-tsî-on-nay kar-tach-ki.

260. Nationality?   Национальность?   *Na-tsî-a-nal'-nast'?*

261. Citizenship?   Гражданство?   *Grazh-dans-tva?*

262. I am an American citizen.   Я американский гражданин.
Ya a-mi-ri-kan-skiy grazh-da-nin.

263. I am... American.   Я... Американец.
Ya... A-mi-ri-ka-nits.

Canadian.   Канадец.   *Ka-na-dits.*

British.   Англичанин.   *An-gli-cha-nin.*

French.   Француз.   *Fran-tsuz.*

264. Occupation?   Профессия?   *Pra-fye-si-ya?*

265. I am... an attorney.   Я... адвокат.   *Ya... a-dva-kat.*

266. Purpose of trip?   Цель поездки?   *Tsel' pa-yest-ki?*

267. I am a tourist.   Я турист.   *Ya tu-rist.*

268. I'm on a business trip.   Я в командиро́вке.
Ya fka-man-di-rof-kye.

269. Length of stay?   Срок пребыва́ния?
Srok pri-by-va-nya?

270. A few days.   Не́сколько дней.   *Nyes-kal'-ka dnyey.*

271. Two weeks.   Две неде́ли.   *Dvye ni-dye-li.*

272. Address in Moscow?   А́дрес в Москве́?
A-dris vMask-vye?

273. Permanent address?   Постоя́нный а́дрес?
Pas-ta-yan-niy a-dris?

AT CUSTOMS

274. What is in here?   Что здесь?   *Shto zdyes'?*

275. Only personal belongings.   То́лько ли́чные ве́щи.
Tol'-ka lich-nî-ye vye-schi.

276. Do I have to declare this?   Это ну́жно деклари́ровать?
E-ta nuzh-na di-kla-ri-ra-vat'?

277. I have nothing to declare.   Мне не́чего деклари́ровать.
Mnye nye-chi-va di-kla-ri-ra-vat'.

278. Do you have this form in English?
У вас есть эта фо́рма на англи́йском языке́?
U-vas yest' e-ta for-ma na-an-gli-skam yi-zî-kye?

Chapter 3
Shopping and Banking

SHOPPING BASICS

279. What kind of store is this?   Какой это магазин?
Ka-_koy_ _e_-ta ma-ga-_zin_?

280. This is a… department store.   Это… универмаг.
_E_-ta… u-ni-vir-_mak_.

deli.   гастроном.   **gas-tra-_nom_.**

grocery store.   продуктовый.   **pra-duk-_to_-viy.**

shoe store.   обувной.   **a-buv-_noy_.**

bookstore.   книжный.   **_knizh_-niy.**

jewelry store.   ювелирный.   **yu-vi-_lir_-niy.**

clothing store.   магазин одежды.
ma-ga-_zin_ a-_dyezh_-di.

electronics store.   магазин электроники.
ma-ga-_zin_ e-lik-_tro_-ni-ki.

hardware store.   хозтовары.   **hos-ta-_va_-rî.**

bank.   банк.   **bank.**

post office.   почта.   **_poch_-ta.**

hair salon.   парикмахерская.   **pa-rik-_ma_-hir-ska-ya.**

dry cleaners.   химчистка.   **him-_chist_-ka.**

laundry.   прачечная.   **_pra_-chish-na-ya.**

pharmacy.   аптека.   **ap-_tye_-ka.**

281. I'd like to buy…   Я хочу́ купи́ть…
Ya ha-_chu_ ku-_pit'_…

282. Can I help you?   Вам помо́чь?   **Vam pa-_moch_?**

283. Yes, please.   Да, пожа́луйста.   **Da, pa-_zha_-lus-ta.**

284. No, thank you.   Нет, спаси́бо.   **Nyet, spa-_si_-ba.**

285. What are you looking for?   Что вас интересу́ет?
Shto vas in-ti-ri-_su_-yit?

286. Please show me that.   Покажи́те вот э́то, пожа́луйста.
Pa-ka-_zhî_-tye vot _e_-ta, pa-_zha_-lus-ta.

287. Can I see this?   Мо́жно посмотре́ть?
Mozh-na pas-ma-_tryet'_?

288. Can I taste this?   Мо́жно попро́бовать?
Mozh-na pa-_pro_-ba-vat'?

289. Can I try it on?   Мо́жно поме́рить?
Mozh-na pa-_mye_-rit'?

290. How much does it cost?   Ско́лькоэ́то сто́ит?
Skol'-ka _e_-ta _sto_-it?

291. One ruble / dollar / euro.   Оди́н рубль / до́ллар / е́вро.
A-_din_ rubl' / _do_-lar / _ye_-vra.

292. Five rubles / dollars / euros.
Пять рубле́й / до́лларов / е́вро.
Pyat' ru-_bley_ / _do_-la-raf / _ye_-vra.

293. Are taxes included?   Нало́ги включены́?
Na-_lo_-gi fklyu-chi-_nî_?

294. This is (very) expensive / cheap.
Э́то (о́чень) до́рого / дёшево.
_E_-ta (_o_-chin') _do_-ra-ga / _dyo_-shi-va.

295. Could we go lower?   Мо́жно деше́вле?
Mozh-na di-_shev_-lye?

296. Do you have anything else?   У вас нет ничегó другóго?
U-_vas_ nyet ni-chi-_vo_ dru-_go_-va?

297. Give me that, please.   Дáйте, пожáлуйста, вот э́то.
Day-tye, pa-_zha_-lus-ta, vot _e_-ta.

298. Please give me… two.   Дáйте, пожáлуйста… две.
Day-tye, pa-_zha_-lus-ta… dvye.

   three.   три.   **_tri._**

   four of them.   четы́ре шту́ки.   **chi-_ti_-rye _shtu_-ki.**

   ten of them.   дéсять штук.   **_dye_-sit' shtuk.**

299. Wrap it, please.   Заверни́те, пожáлуйста.
Za-vir-_ni_-tye, pa-_zha_-lus-ta.

300. It's a gift.   Э́то в подáрок.   **_E_-ta fpa-_da_-rak.**

301. That is all, thank you.   Э́то всё, спаси́бо.
_E_-ta fsyo, spa-_si_-ba.

302. Where do I pay?   Где плати́ть?   **Gdye pla-_tit'_?**

303. Do I pay you?   Плати́ть вам?   **Pla-_tit'_ vam?**

304. Where is the checkout?   Где кáсса?   **Gdye _kas_-sa?**

305. Do you accept… credit?   Вы принимáете… креди́тку?
Vî pri-ni-_may_-tye… kri-_dit_-ku?

   cash.   нали́чные.   **na-_lich_-nî-ye.**

   dollars.   дóллары.   **_do_-la-rî.**

   euro.   éвро.   **_ye_-vra.**

306. Cash only.   Тóлько нали́чные.   **_Tol'_-ka na-_lich_-nî-ye.**

307. Please give me… change.   Дáйте, пожáлуйста… сдáчу.
Day-tye, pa-_zha_-lus-ta… _zda_-chu.

   a receipt.   чек.   **chek.**

308. You didn't count correctly.   Вы непрáвильно посчитáли.
Vî ni-_pra_-vil'-na pa-schi-_ta_-li.

309. I gave you 200 rubles, and you gave me back 25 rubles.
Я вам дал двéсти рублéй, а вы мне дáли двáдцать пять

рублéй сдáчи.
Ya vam dal dvye-sti ru-bley, a vî mnye da-li dva-tsat' pyat'
ru-bley zda-chi.

310. I want to… return this.   Я хочý… вернýть э́то.
Ya ha-chu… vir-nut' e-ta.

exchange…   обменя́ть…   *ab-mi-nyat'…*

311. Here is the receipt.   Вот чек.   *Vot chek.*

312. The store is… closed.   Магази́н… закры́т.
Ma-ga-zin… za-krit.

open.   откры́т.   *at-krit.*

313. When does the store open / close?
Когда́ магази́н открыва́ется / закрыва́ется?
Kag-da ma-ga-zin at-krî-va-yit-sa / za-krî-va-yit-sa?

314. At 7.   В семь часо́в.   *Fsyem' cha-sof.*

315. Are you open… tomorrow?   Вы откры́ты… за́втра?
Vî at-krî-tî… zaf-tra?

on Sunday.   в воскресе́нье.   *vva-skri-sye-nye.*

on weekends.   по выходны́м.   *pa-vî-had-nîm.*

316. Are you in line?   Вы в о́череди?   *Vî vo-chi-ri-di?*

317. Who's last (in line)?   Кто после́дний?
Kto pa-slyed-niy?

318. What are they selling here?   Что здесь даю́т?
Shto zdyes' da-yut?

GROCERIES

319. Where can I buy… fruit?   Где мо́жно купи́ть… фру́кты?
Gdye mozh-na ku-pit'… fruk-tî?

vegetables.   о́вощи.   *o-va-schi.*

320. At a market.   На ры́нке.   *Na rîn-kye.*

321. What can I buy in a deli?
Что мо́жно купи́ть в гастроно́ме?
Shto <u>mozh</u>-na ku-<u>pit'</u> vga-stra-<u>no</u>-mye?

322. Meat, fish, dairy products, eggs.
Мя́со, ры́бу, моло́чные проду́кты, я́йца.
<u>Mya</u>-sa, <u>rî</u>-bu, ma-<u>loch</u>-nî-ye pra-<u>duk</u>-tî, <u>yay</u>-tsa.

323. What about bread or cake?   А хлеб и́ли пиро́г?
A hlyep <u>i</u>-li pi-<u>rok</u>?

324. At a bakery.   В бу́лочной.   *<u>Vbu</u>-lach-nay.*

325. Do you have… rye bread?   У вас есть… чёрный хлеб?
U-vas yest'… <u>chor</u>-nîy hlyep?

chocolate candy.   шокола́дные конфе́ты.
she-ka-<u>lad</u>-nî-ye kan-<u>fye</u>-tî.

raspberry preserves.   клубни́чное варе́нье.
klub-<u>nich</u>-na-ye va-<u>ryen</u>'-ye.

326. Please give me… 200 grams of cheese.
Да́йте, пожа́луйста… две́сти грамм сы́ра.
<u>Day</u>-tye, pa-<u>zha</u>-lus-ta… <u>dvye</u>-sti gram <u>sî</u>-ra.

(half) kilo of ham.   (пол)кило́ ветчины́.
(pol) ki-<u>lo</u> vit-chi-<u>nî</u>.

ten eggs.   деся́ток яи́ц.   *di-<u>sya</u>-tak ya-<u>its</u>.*

a package of tea.   па́чку ча́я.   *<u>pach</u>-ku <u>cha</u>-ya.*

a jar of caviar.   ба́нку икры́.   *<u>ban</u>-ku i-<u>krî</u>.*

a box of candy.   коро́бку конфе́т.   *ka-<u>rop</u>-ku kan-<u>fyet</u>.*

a loaf of bread.   буха́нку хле́ба.   *bu-<u>han</u>-ku <u>hlye</u>-ba.*

a bottle of (carbonated) water.
буты́лку (газиро́ванной) воды́.
bu-<u>tîl</u>-ku (ga-zi-<u>ro</u>-va-nay) va-<u>dî</u>.

327. A bit… more.   Чуть… бо́льше.   *Chut'… <u>bol</u>'-she.*

less.   ме́ньше.   *<u>myen</u>'-she.*

328. Enough.   Хва́тит.   *<u>Hva</u>-tit.*

329. Slice it, please.   Поре́жьте, пожа́луйста.
Pa-ryesh-tye, pa-zha-lus-ta.

330. In one piece.   Одни́м куско́м.   **Ad-nim kus-kom.**

331. Is the fish fresh or frozen?
Ры́ба све́жая и́ли моро́женая?
Ri-ba svye-zha-ya i-li ma-ro-zhî-na-ya?

332. I'll take… a filet.   Я возьму́… филе́.
Ya vaz'-mu… fi-lye.

a steak.   стейк.   **steyk.**

that piece over there.   вот э́тот кусо́к.
vot e-tat ku-sok.

333. Two pieces.   Два куска́.   **Dva kus-ka.**

334. Are the tomatoes ripe?   Помидо́ры спе́лые?
Pa-mi-do-rî spye-lî-ye?

335. Give me ten of them, please.
Да́йте де́сять штук, пожа́луйста.
Day-tye dye-sit' shtuk, pa-zha-lus-ta.

336. Are the apples sweet or tart?
Я́блоки сла́дкие и́ли ки́слые?
Ya-bla-ki slat-ki-ye i-li kis-li-ye?

337. Is the bread fresh?
Хлеб све́жий?
Hlyep svye-zhîy?

338. Half a loaf of rye bread, two croissants, and that pastry.
Пол буха́нки чёрного хле́ба, два рожка́, и вот э́то
пиро́жное.
*Pol bu-han-ki chor-na-va hlye-ba, dva rash-ka i vot e-ta
pi-rozh-na-ye.*

NEWSSTAND, STATIONERY, BOOKSTORE, MUSIC AND VIDEO

339. Do you have… newspapers in English?

У вас есть… газе́ты на англи́йском?
U-vas yest'… ga-zye-tî na-an-gli-skam?

magazines.   журна́лы.   *zhur-na-li.*

books.   кни́ги.   *kni-gi.*

travel guides.   путеводи́тели.   *pu-ti-va-di-ti-li.*

postcards.   откры́тки.   *at-krît-ki.*

postage stamps.   почто́вые ма́рки.
pach-to-vî-ye mar-ki.

a map of the city.   ка́рта го́рода.   *kar-ta go-ra-da.*

souvenirs.   сувени́ры.   *su-vi-ni-rî.*

blank notebooks.   чи́стые тетра́ди.
chis-tî-ye ti-tra-di.

notepads.   блокно́ты.   *blak-no-tî.*

pens.   ру́чки.   *ruch-ki.*

pencils.   карандаши́.   *ka-ran-da-shî.*

Belomor cigarettes.   сигаре́ты Беломо́р.
si-ga-rye-tî Bi-la-mor.

matches.   спи́чки.   *spich-ki.*

a lighter.   зажига́лка.   *za-zhî-gal-ka.*

phone cards.   телефо́нные ка́рточки.
ti-li-fon-nî-ye kar-tach-ki.

CDs by the band Kino.   ди́ски гру́ппы Кино́.
dis-ki gru-pî Ki-no.

films by Sokurov.   фи́льмы Соку́рова.
fil'-mî Sa-ku-ra-va.

340. What region is this for?   На како́й э́то регио́н?
Na ka-koy e-ta ri-gi-on?

341. Is it PAL?   Э́то на систе́му ПАЛ?
E-ta na-sis-tye-mu Pal?

SECAM.   СЕКАМ.   *Si-kam.*

NTSC?   NTSC?   *NTSC?*

342. Does it have English subtitles?
     Здесь есть английские субтитры?
     Zdyes' yest' an-gli-ski-ye sup-ti-trî?

CLOTHES AND SHOES

343. I need a... shirt. (f.)   Мне нужна... рубашка.
     Mnye nuzh-na... ru-bash-ka.

     t-shirt.   футболка.   *fud-bol-ka.*

     skirt.   юбка.   *yup-ka.*

     jacket.   куртка.   *kurt-ka.*

     fur coat.   шуба.   *shu-ba.*

     hat.   шапка.   *shap-ka.*

344. I need a... sweater. (m.)   Мне нужен... свитер.
     Mnye nu-zhîn... svi-ter.

     suit.   костюм.   *kas-tyum.*

     sports jacket. пиджак.   *pid-zhak.*

     tie.   галстук.   *gal-stuk.*

     bathing suit. купальник.   *ku-pal'-nik.*

     bra.   лифчик.   *lif-chik.*

345. I need... pants. (pl.)   Мне нужны... брюки.
     Mnye nuzh-nî... bryu-ki.

     shorts.   шорты.   *shor-tî.*

     stockings.   чулки.   *chul-ki.*

     swimming trunks. плавки.   *plaf-ki.*

     underpants.   трусы.   *tru-sî.*

     shoes.   туфли.   *tuf-li.*

     ankle boots.   ботинки.   *ba-tin-ki.*

     boots.   сапоги.   *sa-pa-gi.*

     slippers.   тапочки.   *ta-pach-ki.*

     flip-flops.   вьетнамки.   *vyet-nam-ki.*

     socks.   носки.   *nas-ki.*

346. I need… a winter coat.   Мне ну́жно… зи́мнее пальто́.
Mnye <u>nuzh</u>-na… <u>zim</u>-ni-ye pal'-<u>to</u>.

underwear.   ни́жнее бельё.   *nizh-ni-ye bil'-<u>yo</u>.*

bedding.   посте́льное бельё.   *pas-<u>tel</u>'-na-ye bil'-<u>yo</u>.*

347. Men's or women's?   Мужски́е и́ли же́нские?
Mush-<u>ski</u>-ye i-li <u>zhen</u>-ski-ye?

348. What color?   Како́го цве́та?   *Ka-<u>ko</u>-va <u>tsvye</u>-ta?*

349. Black, white, gray…   Чёрные, бе́лые, се́рые…
Chor-nî-ye, <u>bye</u>-li-ye, <u>sye</u>-rî-ye…

350. What is your… shoe size?   Како́й у вас разме́р… ноги́?
Ka-<u>koy</u> u-<u>vas</u> raz-<u>myer</u>… na-gi?

waist.   та́лии.   *<u>ta</u>-li-i.*

chest.   груди́.   *gru-<u>di</u>.*

head.   головы́.   *ga-la-<u>vî</u>.*

neck.   ше́и.   *<u>she</u>-i.*

clothing.   оде́жды.   *a-<u>dyezh</u>-dî.*

351. My shoe size is… forty-two (European).
Разме́р ноги́… со́рок второ́й (европе́йский).
Raz-<u>myer</u> na-gi… <u>so</u>-rak fta-<u>roy</u> (yi-vra-<u>pyey</u>-skiy).

nine (U.S.).   девя́тый (США).   *di-<u>vya</u>-tîy (S-sha).*

352. My waist size is… thirty inches.
Разме́р та́лии… три́дцать дю́ймов.
Raz-<u>myer</u> <u>ta</u>-li-i… <u>tri</u>-tsat' <u>dyuy</u>-maf.

seventy-six cm.   се́мдесят шесть сантиме́тров.
syem-di-sit shest' san-ti-<u>myet</u>-raf.

353. Where is the mirror?   Где здесь зе́ркало?
Gdey zdyes' <u>zyer</u>-ka-la?

354. Where can I try it on?   Где мо́жно приме́рить?
Gdye <u>mozh</u>-na pri-<u>mye</u>-rit'?

355. This does not fit.   Э́то не подхо́дит.
<u>E</u>-ta ni-pat-<u>ho</u>-dit.

356. I (don't) like this.   Это мне (не) нра́вится.
E-ta mnye (ni-) nra-vit-sya.

357. This is too… big.   Это мне… велико́.
E-ta mnye… vi-li-ko.

small.   ма́ло.   **ma-lo.**

358. Do you have a bigger / smaller size?
У вас есть бо́льший / ме́ньший разме́р?
U-vas yest' bol'-shîy / myen'-shîy raz-myer?

359. This is a small, and I need a… medium.
Это ма́ленький разме́р, а мне ну́жен… сре́дний.
E-ta ma-lin'-kiy raz-myer, a-mnye nu-zhîn… sryed-niy.

large.   большо́й.   **bal'-shoy.**

360. I'll think about it.   Я поду́маю.
Ya pa-du-ma-yu.

PHARMACY

361. Can you please tell me where I can find a pharmacy?
Скажи́те, пожа́луйста, где апте́ка?
Ska-zhî-tye, pa-zha-lus-ta, gdye ap-tye-ka?

362. Is there a 24-hour pharmacy near here?
Где́-нибудь есть круглосу́точная апте́ка?
Gdye-ni-but' yest' kru-gla-su-tach-na-ya ap-tye-ka?

363. I need medication for… a cough.
Мне ну́жно лека́рство от… ка́шля.
Mnye nuzh-na li-kar-stva at… kash-lya.

runny nose.   на́сморка.   **nas-mar-ka.**

fever.   температу́ры.   **tim-pi-ra-tu-rî.**

headache.   головно́й бо́ли.   **ga-lav-noy bo-li.**

joint pain.   бо́ли в суста́вах.   **bo-li fsu-sta-vah.**

allergy.   аллерги́и.   **a-lir-gi-i.**

heartburn.   изжо́ги.   **iz-zho-gi.**

364. I've run out of medication.   У меня ко́нчилось лека́рство.
U-mi-nya kon-chi-las' li-kar-stva.

365. Do you have this medication?   У вас есть э́то лека́рство?
U-vas yest' e-ta li-kar-stva?

366. Here's the prescription.   Вот реце́пт.   *Vot ri-tsept.*

367. When should I take this medication?
Когда́ принима́ть лека́рство?
Kag-da pri-ni-mat' li-kar-stva?

368. How many times a day?   Ско́лько раз в день?
Skol'-ka raz vdyen'?

369. Can I drink alcohol?   Мо́жно пить алкого́ль?
Mozh-na pit' al-ka-gol'?

370. Can I drive?   Мо́жно води́ть маши́ну?
Mozh-na va-dit' ma-shî-nu?

371. Where do you keep… aspirin?   Где у вас… аспири́н?
Gdye u-vas… as-pi-rin?

bandages.   пла́стыри.   *plas-tî-ri.*

sleeping pills.   снотво́рное.   *sna-tvor-na-ye.*

laxatives.   слаби́тельное.   *sla-bi-til'-na-ye.*

vitamins.   витами́ны.   *vi-ta-mi-nî.*

contact lens solution.   жи́дкость для конта́ктных линз.
zhît-kast' dlya kan-takt-nîh lins.

condoms.   презервати́вы.   *pri-zir-va-ti-vî.*

sanitary pads.   гигиени́ческие прокла́дки.
gi-gi-yi-ni-chis-ki-ye pra-klat-ki.

tampons.   тампо́ны.   *tam-po-nî.*

ELECTRONICS, PHOTO AND VIDEO

372. I would like to buy a… digital / film camera.
Я хочу купить… цифровой / плёночный фотоаппарат.
Ya ha-<u>chu</u> ku-<u>pit'</u>… tsîf-ra-<u>voy</u> / <u>plyo</u>-nach-nîy fo-ta-a-pa-<u>rat</u>.

video camera.   видеокамеру.   *vi-di-a-<u>ka</u>-mi-ru.*

lens.   объектив.   *ab-yik-<u>tif</u>.*

373. I need… color film for this camera.
Мне нужна… цветная фотоплёнка для этого аппарата.
Mnye nuzh-<u>na</u>… tsvit-<u>na</u>-ya fo-ta-<u>plyon</u>-ka dlya <u>e</u>-ta-va a-pa-<u>ra</u>-ta.

black-and-white.   чернобелая.   *chir-na-<u>bye</u>-la-ya.*

slide.   слайдовая.   *<u>slay</u>-da-va-ya.*

a USB flash drive.   флёшка.   *<u>flesh</u>-ka.*

an SD, SxS card.   карточка SD, SxS.
<u>kar</u>-tach-ka SD, SxS.

videocassette (DV, miniDV).   видеокассета (ДВ миниДВ).
vi-di-a-ka-<u>sye</u>-ta (de-<u>ve</u>, <u>mi</u>-ni-de-<u>ve</u>).

374. I need a charger for… a mobile phone.
Мне нужна зарядка для… мобильного.
Mnye nuzh-<u>na</u> za-<u>ryat</u>-ka dlya… ma-<u>bil'</u>-na-va.

photo camera.   фотоаппарата.   *fo-ta-a-pa-<u>ra</u>-ta.*

video camera.   видеокамеры.   *vi-di-a-<u>ka</u>-mi-ri.*

laptop.   ноутбука.   *no-ut-<u>bu</u>-ka.*

375. Do you have… a plug adaptor?
У вас есть… переходник для розетки?
U-<u>vas</u> yest'… pi-ri-had-<u>nik</u> dlya ra-<u>zyet</u>-ki?

a USB cable.   провод USB (ю-эс-би).
pro-<u>vat</u> yu-es-<u>bi</u>.

batteries (for a photo camera).
батарейки (для фотоаппарата).
ba-ta-<u>ryey</u>-ki (dlya fo-ta-a-pa-<u>ra</u>-ta).

376. Can I … develop film here?
Здесь мо́жно… прояви́ть фотоплёнку?
Zdyes' mozh-na… pra-i-vit' fo-ta-plyon-ku?

print (digital) photos.
отпеча́тать (цифровы́е) фотосни́мки.
at-pi-cha-tat' (tsîf-ra-vî-ye) fo-ta-snim-ki.

377. Please show me… mobile phones.
Покажи́те, пожа́луйста… моби́льные телефо́ны.
Pa-ka-zhî-tye, pa-zha-lus-ta… ma-bil'-nî-ye ti-li-fo-nî.

laptops.   ноутбу́ки.   *no-ut-bu-ki.*

MP3 players.   MP3-плéеры.   *em-pe-tri ple-i-rî.*

headphones.   нау́шники.   *na-ush-ni-ki.*

BANKING AND CURRENCY EXCHANGE

378. Tell me, is there… a bank around here?
Скажи́те, где здесь… банк?
Ska-zhî-tye, gdye zdyes'… bank?

an ATM.   банкома́т.   *ban-ka-mat.*

a currency exchange.   обме́н валю́ты.
ab-myen va-lyu-tî.

379. Which bank do you need?   Како́й банк вам ну́жен?
Ka-koy bank vam nu-zhîn?

380. It doesn't matter.   Не ва́жно.   *Ni-vazh-na.*

381. Any (bank).   Любо́й (банк).   *Lyu-boy (bank).*

382. I need to withdraw money… from an account.
Мне ну́жно снять де́ньги… со счёта.
Mnye nuzh-na snyat' dyen'-gi… sa-schyo-ta.

as a cash advance on a credit card.
по креди́тной ка́рточке.
pa-kri-dit-nay kar-tach-kye.

383. Would you like rubles or dollars?
Вы хоти́те получи́ть рубли́ и́ли до́ллары?
Vî ha-ti-tye pa-lu-chit' rub-li i-li do-la-rî?

384. Rubles, please.   Рубли, пожалуйста.
Rub-_li_, pa-_zha_-lus-ta.

385. How much do you need?   Сколько вам нужно?
Skol'-ka vam _nuzh_-na?

386. Here is my card.   Вот моя карточка.
Vot ma-_ya_ _kar_-tach-ka.

387. Is this a debit or credit card?
Это карточка кредитная или дебитная?
_E_-ta _kar_-tach-ka kri-_dit_-na-ya _i_-li de-_bit_-na-ya?

388. Please show your passport.   Покажите ваш паспорт.
Pa-ka-_zhî_-tye vash _pas_-port.

389. Please enter your PIN number.
Введите ваш код, пожалуйста.
Vvi-_di_-tye vash kot, pa-_zha_-lus-ta.

390. Small bills, please.   Мелкими купюрами, пожалуйста.
Myel-ki-mi ku-_pyu_-ra-mi, pa-_zha_-lus-ta.

391. Your ATM isn't working.   Ваш банкомат не работает.
Vash ban-ka-_mat_ ni-ra-_bo_-ta-it.

392. What's the problem?   В чём дело?   **Fchom _dye_-la?**

393. The ATM has not returned my card.
Банкомат не отдаёт мою карточку.
Ban-ka-_mat_ ni-at-da-_yot_ ma-_yu_ _kar_-tach-ku.

394. The ATM has not dispensed my money.
Банкомат не выдаёт деньги.
Ban-ka-_mat_ ni-vî-da-_yot_ _dyen_'-gi.

395. Can I exchange money here?
Здесь можно обменять деньги?
Zdyes' _mozh_-na ab-mi-_nyat_' _dyen_'-gi?

396. Can you exchange… dollars for rubles?
     Вы мóжете обменя́ть… дóллары на рубли́?
     Vî <u>mo</u>-zhî-tye ab-mi-<u>nyat'</u>… <u>do</u>-la-rî na-ru-<u>bli</u>?

     rubles for dollars.   рубли́ на дóллары.
     ru <u>bli</u> na-<u>do</u>-la-rî.

     for euro.   на éвро.   *na-<u>yev</u>-ra.*

397. What is your exchange rate?   Какóй у вас курс?
     Ka-<u>koy</u> u-<u>vas</u> kurs?

Chapter 4
Accommodations

HOTEL BASICS

398. Where are you staying?   Где вы остановились?
    Gdye vî as-ta-na-__vi__-lis'?

399. We are staying… at the Hotel Metropol.
    Мы остановились… в гостинице Метрополь.
    Mî as-ta-na-__vi__-lis'… vgas-__ti__-ni-tse Mi-tra-__pol__'.

    with friends.   у друзей.   *u-dru-__zyey__.*

    at a private home.   на частной квартире.
    na __chas__-nay kvar-__ti__-rye.

400. Could you recommend a… hotel?
    Вы можете рекомендовать… гостиницу?
    Vî __mo-zhî__-tye ri-ka-min-da-__vat__'… gas-__ti__-ni-tsu?

    hostel.   хостел.   *__hos__-tel.*

401. It's not too expensive?   Это не дорого?
    __E__-ta ni-__do__-ra-ga?

402. Three thousand rubles per night.
    Три тысячи рублей за ночь.
    Tri __ti__-si-chi rub-__lyey__ __za__-nach.

RESERVING A ROOM

403. Hello, I need a room.   Здравствуйте, мне нужен номер.
Zdras-tvuy-tye, mnye _nu_-zhîn _no_-mir.

404. I'm sorry, we have no rooms available.
Извините, у нас нет свободных номеров.
Iz-vi-_ni_-tye, u-_nas_ nyet sva-_bod_-nîh na-mi-_rof_.

405. For how many people?   На сколько человек?
Na-_skol'_-ka chi-la-_vyek_?

406. For... one.   На... одного.   **Na-... ad-na-_vo_.**
two.   двоих.   **dva-_ih_.**
three.   троих.   **tra-_ih_.**

407. For two with a child.   На двоих с ребёнком.
Na-dva-_ih_ sri-_byon_-kam.

408. There are four of us.   Нас четверо.   **Nas _chet_-vi-ra.**

409. We have two children with us.   С нами двое детей.
Sna-mi _dvo_-ye di-_tyey_.

410. For how many nights?   На сколько ночей?
Na-_skol'_-ka na-_chey_?

411. For... one night.   На... одну ночь.   **Na-... ad-_nu_ noch.**
two nights.   две ночи.   **dvye _no_-chi.**
five nights.   пять ночей.   **pyat' na-_chey_.**

412. How many beds are in the room?
Сколько кроватей в номере?
Skol'-ka kra-_va_-tyey _vno_-mi-rye?

413. The room has one double bed and two single beds.
В номере одна двуспальная кровать и две односпальные.
**_Vno_-mi-rye ad-_na_ dvu-_spal'_-na-ya kra-_vat'_ i-_dvye_
ad-na-_spal'_-nî-ye.**

414. Is there a... toilet in the room?   В номере есть... туалет?
Vno-mi-rye yest'... tu-a-_lyet_?

shower.   душ.   *dush.*

kitchen.   ку́хня.   *kuh-nya.*

AC.   кондиционе́р.   *kan-di-tsî-a-nyer.*

television.   телеви́зор.   *ti-li-vi-zar.*

Internet.   интерне́т.   *in-ter-net.*

415. Toilet and shower are separate, in the hallway.
Туале́т и душ отде́льно, на этаже́.
Tu-a-lyet i-dush at-del'-na, na-e-ta-zhe.

416. There is hot water only in the morning.
Горя́чая вода́ то́лько по утра́м.
Ga-rya-cha-ya va-da tol'-ka pa-ut-ram.

417. Which floor is the room on?   На како́м этаже́ но́мер?
Na-ka-kom e-ta-zhe no-mir?

418. Is it ever noisy in the room?   В но́мере быва́ет шу́мно?
Vno-mi-rye bî-va-it shum-na?

419. May I smoke in the room?   В но́мере мо́жно кури́ть?
Vno-mi-rye mozh-na ku-rit'?

420. How much is it per night?   Ско́лько э́то сто́ит за́ ночь?
Skol'-ka e-ta sto-it za-nach?

421. Do you have anything cheaper?
У вас нет ничего́ подеше́вле?
U-vas nyet ni-chi-vo pa-di-shev-lye?

422. Do you accept dollars?   Вы принима́ете до́ллары?
Vî pri-ni-may-tye do-la-rî?

423. Can I see the room?   Мо́жно посмотре́ть но́мер?
Mozh-na pas-mat-ryet' no-mir?

424. Is breakfast included?   За́втрак включён?
Zaf-trak fklyu-chon?

425. What time is check-out?   В кото́ром часу́ вы́езд?
Fka-to-ram cha-su vî-yist?

CHECKING IN AND OUT

426. I've reserved a room.   Я брони́ровал но́мер.
Ya bra-ni-ra-val no-mir.

427. Here are my documents.   Вот мои́ докуме́нты.
Vot ma-i da-ku-myen-tî.

428. Please fill out this form.
Пожа́луйста, запо́лните ка́рту го́стя.
Pa-zha-lus-ta, za-pol-ni-tye kar-tu gos-tya.

429. Do you have forms in English?
У вас есть бла́нки на англи́йском?
U-vas yest' blan-ki na-an-glis-kam?

430. You owe five thousand rubles.   С вас пять ты́сяч рубле́й.
Svas pyat' ti-sich rub-ley.

431. I've already paid.   Я уже́ плати́л.   *Ya u-zhe pla-til.*

432. Here is a confirmation.   Вот подтвержде́ние.
Vot pa-tvir-zhdye-nye.

433. Here is the key to your room.
Пожа́луйста, ключ от но́мера.
Pa-zha-lus-ta, klyuch at-no-mi-ra.

434. I would like to stay an extra… night.
Я хочу́ оста́ться ещё на… одну́ ночь.
Ya ha-chu as-tat'-sya yi-scho na… ad-nu noch.

two nights.   две но́чи.   *dvye no-chi.*

a week.   неде́лю.   *ni-dye-lyu.*

435. Where can I leave my luggage?
Где мо́жно оста́вить бага́ж?
Gdye mozh-na as-ta-vit' ba-gash?

436. Leave your things here.   Оста́вьте ве́щи здесь.
As-taf'-tye vye-schi zdyes'.

SERVICES AND COMPLAINTS

437. Pardon me, where is the... cafeteria?
Извините, где здесь... буфёт?
Iz-vi-ni-tye, gdye zdyes'... bu-fyet?

restaurant.   рестора́н.   *ris-ta-ran.*

gym.   спортза́л.   *sport-zal.*

swimming pool.   бассе́йн.   *ba-seyn.*

438. What time is breakfast?   В кото́ром часу́ за́втрак?
Fka-to-ram cha-su zaf-trak?

439. Is there laundry service here?   Здесь есть пра́чечная?
Zdyes' yest' pra-chish-na-ya?

440. Please change the sheets in my room.
Пожа́луйста, поменя́йте бельё в но́мере.
Pa-zha-lus-ta, pa-mi-nyay-tye bil'-yo vno-mi-rye.

441. The room is missing... a blanket.   В но́мере нет... одея́ла.
Vno-mi-rye nyet... a-di-ya-la.

pillows.   поду́шек.   *pa-du-shîk.*

sheets.   про́стынь.   *pros-tin'.*

toilet paper.   туале́тной бума́ги.
tu-a-lyet-nay bu-ma-gi.

442. The room is (very)... cold.   В но́мере (о́чень)... хо́лодно.
Vno-mi-rye (o-chin')... ho-lad-na.

hot.   жа́рко.   *zhar-ka.*

noisy.   шу́мно.   *shum-na.*

443. My room only has cold water.
У меня́ в но́мере то́лько холо́дная вода́.
U-mi-nya vno-mi-rye tol'-ka ha-lod-na-ya va-da.

444. My... refrigerator isn't working.
В но́мере не рабо́тает... холоди́льник.
Vno-mi-rye ni-ra-bo-ta-it... ha-la-dil'-nik.

television.   телеви́зор.   *ti-li-vi-zar.*

fan.   вентилятор.   *vin-ti-lya-tar.*

445. There is a bad smell in the room.   В номере плохо пахнет.
Vno-mi-rye plo-ha pah-nit.

446. Can I make an international call from my room?
Я могу сделать международный звонок из номера?
Ya ma-gu zdye-lat' mizh-du-na-rod-niy zva-nok iz-no-mi-ra?

ANSWERING THE DOOR

447. Who is it?   Кто там?   *Kto tam?*

448. Wait!   Подождите!   *Pa-dazh-di-tye!*

449. One moment!   Одну минуту!   *Ad-nu mi-nu-tu!*

450. Come in!   Заходите!   *Za-ha-di-tye!*

RENTING AND HOMESTAY

451. Are you renting out… an apartment?
Вы сдаёте… квартиру?
Vî zda-yo-tye… kvar-ti-ru?

room.   комнату.   *kom-na-tu.*

dacha.   дачу.   *da-chu.*

452. I would like to rent an apartment for a week.
Я хочу снять квартиру на неделю.
Ya ha-chu snyat' kvar-ti-ru na-ni-dye-lyu.

453. Is the apartment far from the city center?
Квартира далеко от центра?
Kvar-ti-ra da-li-ko at-tsen-tra?

454. Is there a… metro nearby?   Рядом есть… метро?
Rya-dam yest'… mit-ro?

bus stop.   остановка автобуса.
as-ta-nof-ka af-to-bu-sa.

Internet café.   интернет-кафе.   *in-ter-net ka-fe.*

grocery store.   продукто́вый.   *pra-duk-to-viy.*

455. Is there a washing machine in the apartment?
В кварти́ре есть стира́льная маши́на?
Fkvar-ti-rye yest' sti-ral'-na-ya ma-shî-na?

456. Where can I park my car?
Где мо́жно поста́вить маши́ну?
Gdye mozh-na pas-ta-vit' ma-shî-nu?

457. How many... rooms are in the apartment?
Ско́лько... ко́мнат в кварти́ре?
Skol'-ka... kom-nat fkvar-ti-rye?

beds.   крова́тей.   *kra-va-tiy.*

458. Can we use the... kitchen?
Мы мо́жем по́льзоваться... ку́хней?
Mî mo-zhîm pol'-za-vat'-sa... kuh-niy?

washer.   стира́льной маши́ной.   *sti-ral-nay ma-shî-nay.*

television.   телеви́зором.   *ti-li-vi-za-ram.*

parking.   стоя́нкой.   *sta-yan-kay.*

459. How early do you... get up?   Как ра́но вы... встаёте?
Kak ra-na vî fsta-yo-tye?

go to bed.   ложи́тесь.   *la-zhî-tis'.*

460. How many people live in the apartment?
Ско́лько люде́й живёт в кварти́ре?
Skol'-ka lyu-dyey zhî-vyot fkvar-ti-rye?

461. When can we see the apartment?
Когда́ мо́жно посмотре́ть кварти́ру?
Kag-da mozh-na pas-mat-ryet' kvar-ti-ru?

462. Do you live... there?   Вы живёте... там?
Vî zhî-vyo-tye... tam?

nearby.   ря́дом.   *rya-dam.*

463. How can I get in touch with you?
Как мо́жно с ва́ми связа́ться?
Kak <u>mozh</u>-na <u>sva</u>-mi svi-<u>zat</u>'-sa?

Chapter 5
Eating

EATING BASICS

464. I'm (not) hungry.   Я (не) го́лоден *(m.)* / голодна́ *(f.)*
Ya (ni-) go-la-din / ga-lad-_na_.

465. I'd like to… eat something.   Я хочу́… есть.
Ya ha-_chu_… yest'.

drink something.   пить.   **pit'.**

466. Where can we… eat around here?
Где здесь мо́жно… пое́сть?
Gdye zdyes' _mozh_-na… pa-yest'?

drink.   попи́ть.   **pa-_pit_'.**

467. Do you have anything to… eat?
У вас есть что́-нибудь… пое́сть?
U-_vas_ yest' _shto_-ni-but'… pa-_yest_'?

drink.   попи́ть.   **pa-_pit_'.**

468. Is this a restaurant?   Э́то рестора́н?   **E-_ta_ ris-ta-_ran_?**

469. No, this is a… café.   Нет, э́то… кафе́.
Nyet, e-_ta_… ka-_fe_.

cafeteria.   столо́вая.   **sta-_lo_-va-ya.**

bar.   бар.   **bar.**

470. What's for... breakfast? Что на... за́втрак?
Shto na... <u>zaf</u>-trak?

lunch. обе́д. **a-<u>byet</u>.**

dinner. у́жин. **<u>u</u>-zhîn.**

471. Do you have any... soup? У вас есть... суп?
U-<u>vas</u> yest'... sup?

sandwiches. бутербро́ды. **bu-ter-<u>bro</u>-dî.**

omelets. омле́ты. **am-<u>lye</u>-tî.**

salads. сала́ты. **sa-<u>la</u>-tî.**

snacks. заку́ски. **za-<u>kus</u>-ki.**

fish. ры́ба. **<u>rî</u>-ba.**

meat. мя́со. **<u>mya</u>-sa.**

poultry. пти́ца. **<u>pti</u>-tsa.**

hot dishes. горя́чие блю́да. **ga-<u>rya</u>-chi-ye <u>blyu</u>-da.**

vegetable dishes. овощны́е блю́да.
a-vasch-<u>nî</u>-ye <u>blyu</u>-da.

fruit. фру́кты. **<u>fruk</u>-tî.**

caviar. икра́. **i-<u>kra</u>.**

dumplings. пельме́ни. **pil'-<u>mye</u>-ni.**

crêpes. блины́. **bli-<u>nî</u>.**

kabobs. шашлыки́. **shash-lî-<u>ki</u>.**

cutlets. котле́ты. **kat-<u>lye</u>-tî.**

stuffed buns. пирожки́. **pi-rash-<u>ki</u>.**

(buckwheat) porridge. ка́ша. **<u>ka</u>-sha.**

dessert. сла́дкое. **<u>slat</u>-ka-ye.**

ice cream. моро́женое. **ma-<u>ro</u>-zhî-na-ye.**

coffee. ко́фе. **<u>ko</u>-fe.**

kvass. квас. **kvas.**

juice. сок. **sok.**

water. вода́. **va-<u>da</u>.**

beer. пи́во. **<u>pi</u>-va.**

wine.   вино́.   *vi-no.*

vodka.   во́дка.   *vot-ka.*

cognac.   конья́к.   *ka-nyak.*

whiskey. ви́ски.   *vis-ki.*

472. We only have cold appetizers.
У нас то́лько холо́дные заку́ски.
U-nas tol'-ka ha-lod-nî-ye za-kus-ki.

473. The kitchen is closed.   Ку́хня закры́та.
Kuh-nya za-krî-ta.

MAKING RESERVATIONS

474. I'd like to reserve a table for… two.
Я хочу́ заказа́ть сто́лик на… двои́х.
Ya ha-chu za-ka-zat' sto-lik… na-dva-ih.

three.   на трои́х.   *na-tra-ih.*

four.   на четверы́х.   *na-chit-vi-rîh.*

475. For what time?   На кото́рый час?   *Na-ka-to-rîy chas?*

476. For 7 p.m.   На семь ве́чера.   *Na-syem' vye-chi-ra.*

477. Today everything is booked.   Сего́дня всё за́нято.
Si-vod-nya fsyo za-ni-ta.

478. This is for… tomorrow.   Э́то на… за́втра.
E-ta na… zaf-tra.

Saturday.   суббо́ту.   *su-bo-tu.*

the fifth. пя́тое число́. *pya-ta-ye chis-lo.*

479. Under what name?   На чьё и́мя?   *Na-chyo i-mya?*

480. Smoking or non-smoking?   Куря́щий и́ли некуря́щий?
Ku-rya-schiy i-li ni-ku-rya-schiy?

SEATING

481. We had reserved a table for Martin.
Мы зака́зывали сто́лик, на и́мя Ма́ртин.
Mî za-<u>ka</u>-zî-va-li <u>sto</u>-lik, na-i-mya <u>Mar</u>-tin.

482. Do you have a free table?   У вас есть свобо́дный сто́лик?
U-<u>vas</u> yest' sva-<u>bod</u>-nîy <u>sto</u>-lik?

483. The table over there, please.   Вот тот сто́лик, пожа́луйста.
Vot tot <u>sto</u>-lik, pa-<u>zha</u>-lus-ta.

484. Could we sit... on the patio?   Мо́жно... на тера́ссе?
<u>Mozh</u>-na... na-ti-<u>ra</u>-sye?

by the window.   у окна́.   *u-ak-<u>na</u>.*

over there.   вон там.   *von tam.*

ORDERING

485. Waiter! *(m./f.)*   Официа́нт!   *A-fi-tsî-<u>ant</u>!*

486. Please bring... a menu.   Пожа́луйста, принеси́те... меню́.
Pa-<u>zha</u>-lus-ta, pri-ni-<u>si</u>-tye... mi-<u>nyu</u>.

the wine list.   ви́нную ка́рту.   *<u>vin</u>-nu-yu <u>kar</u>-tu.*

487. Do you have a menu in English?
У вас есть меню́ на англи́йском?
U-<u>vas</u> yest' mi-<u>nyu</u> na-an-<u>gli</u>-skam?

488. We are ready to order.   Мы гото́вы зака́зывать.
Mî ga-<u>to</u>-vî za-<u>ka</u>-zî-vat'.

489. What will you be having?   Что вы бу́дете зака́зывать?
Shto vî <u>bu</u>-di-tye za-<u>ka</u>-zî-vat'?

490. What do you recommend?   Что вы рекоменду́ете?
Shto vî ri-ka-min-<u>duy</u>-tye?

491. What are the house specialties?
Каки́е здесь фи́рменные блю́да?
Ka-<u>ki</u>-ye zdyes' <u>fir</u>-mi-nî-ye <u>blyu</u>-da?

492. Is this a vegetarian dish? Это вегетариа́нское блю́до?
E-ta vi-gi-ta-ri-<u>an</u>-ska-ye <u>blyu</u>-da?

493. Do you have any vegetarian dishes?
У вас есть вегетариа́нские блю́да?
U-<u>vas</u> yest' vi-gi-ta-ri-<u>an</u>-ski-ye <u>blyu</u>-da?

494. What's in this? С чем э́то? *S chem <u>e</u>-ta?*

495. What are they having? Что́ это у них?
<u>Shto</u>-e-ta u-<u>nih</u>?

496. For an appetizer... bring us [dish].
На заку́ску... принеси́те...
Na-za-<u>kus</u>-ku... pri-ni-<u>si</u>-tye...

   For the first course... На пе́рвое... *Na-<u>pyer</u>-va-ye...*

   For the second course... На второ́е *Na-fta-<u>ro</u>-ye.*

   For dessert... На десе́рт... *Na-di-<u>syert</u>...*

497. A bowl of soup. Таре́лку су́па. *Ta-<u>ryel</u>-ku <u>su</u>-pa.*

498. What will you drink? Что бу́дете пить?
Shto <u>bu</u>-di-tye pit'?

499. A glass of... (mineral) water.
Стака́н... (минера́льной) воды́.
Sta-<u>kan</u>... (mi-ni-<u>ral</u>'-nay) va-<u>dî</u>.

   beer. пи́ва. *<u>pi</u>-va.*

500. A bottle of... red wine. Буты́лку... кра́сного вина́.
Bu-<u>til</u>-ku... <u>kras</u>-na-va vi-<u>na</u>.

   white wine. бе́лого вина́. *<u>bye</u>-la-va vi-<u>na</u>.*

   champagne. шампа́нского. *sham-<u>pan</u>-ska-va.*

501. A cup of... coffee. Ча́шку... ко́фе.
<u>Chash</u>-ku... <u>ko</u>-fye.

   tea. ча́я. *<u>cha</u>-ya.*

502. Tea with... lemon. Чай с... лимо́ном.
Chay s... li-<u>mo</u>-nam.

   milk. молоко́м. *ma-la-<u>kom</u>.*

   honey. мёдом. *<u>myo</u>-dam.*

503. Something for dessert?   Что́-нибудь на десе́рт?
Shto-ni-but' na-di-syert?

504. Enjoy!   Прия́тного аппети́та!
Pri-yat-na-va a-pi-ti-ta!

PREPARATION

505. How should we cook your... steak?
Как приготовить ваш... стейк?
Kak pri-ga-to-vit' vash... steyk?

hamburger.   га́мбургер.   *gam-bur-gyer.*

506. Rare (lit. "with blood").   С кро́вью.   *Skro-vyu.*

507. Medium. (lit. "half-cooked").   Полу-прожа́ренный.
Po-lu-pra-zha-ri-niy.

508. Welldone.   Прожа́ренный.   *Pra-zha-ri-niy.*

509. Please make it without... garlic.
Пожа́луйста, приготовьте э́то без... чеснока́.
Pa-zha-lus-ta, pri-ga-tof'-tye e-ta bis... chis-na-ka.

pepper.   пе́рца.   *pyer-tsa.*

cheese.   сы́ра.   *si-ra.*

510. I am allergic to... nuts.   У меня́ аллерги́я на... оре́хи.
U-mi-nya a-lir-gi-ya na... a-rye-hi.

peanuts.   ара́хис.   *a-ra-his.*

lactose.   лакто́зу.   *lak-to-zu.*

shellfish.   моллю́ски.   *ma-lyus-ki.*

gluten.   глю́тен.   *glyu-ten.*

511. I don't eat... salty foods.   Я не ем... солёного.
Ya ni-yem... sa-lyo-na-va.

spicy.   о́строго.   *os-tra-va.*

sweet.   сла́дкого.   *slat-ka-va.*

fatty.   жи́рного.   *zhir-na-va.*

dairy.	моло́чного.	*ma-<u>loch</u>-na-va.*
meat.	мя́со.	*<u>mya</u>-sa.*
bread.	хлеб.	*hlyep.*

512. I don't drink alcohol.   Я не пью алкого́ль.
Ya ni-<u>pyu</u> al-ka-<u>gol</u>'.

SERVICE, COMPLAINTS AND COMPLIMENTS

513. Please, more (another)… water.
Пожа́луйста, ещё… воды́.
Pa-<u>zha</u>-lus-ta, yi-<u>scho</u>… va-dî.

bread.	хле́ба.	*<u>hlye</u>-ba.*
wine.	вина́.	*vi-<u>na</u>.*
of this.	вот э́того.	*vot <u>e</u>-ta-va.*
napkin.	салфе́тку.	*sal-<u>fyet</u>-ku.*
spoon.	ло́жку.	*<u>losh</u>-ku.*
fork.	ви́лку.	*<u>vil</u>-ku.*
knife.	нож.	*nosh.*
plate.	таре́лку.	*ta-<u>ryel</u>-ku.*

514. Will it be long?   Ещё до́лго?   *Yi-<u>scho</u> <u>dol</u>-ga?*

515. We've been waiting a long time.   Мы уже́ до́лго ждём.
Mî u-<u>zhe</u> <u>dol</u>-ga zhdyom.

516. What is this?   Что́ это?   *<u>Shto</u>-e-ta?*

517. I didn't order this. *(m./f.)*   Я э́того не зака́зывал(а).
Ya <u>e</u>-ta-va ni-za-<u>ka</u>-zî-val (-a).

518. The food is too… cold.   Еда́ сли́шком… холо́дная.
Yi-<u>da</u> <u>slish</u>-kam… ha-<u>lod</u>-na-ya.

hot.	горя́чая.	*ga-<u>rya</u>-chi-ya.*
spicy.	о́страя.	*<u>ost</u>-ra-ya.*
salty.	солёная.	*sa-<u>lyo</u>-na-ya.*

519. The meat is… raw. Мясо… сырое.
Mya-sa… si-ro-ye.

not fresh. несвежее. *ni-svye-zhî-ye.*

520. There's too little… salt. Мало… соли. *Ma-la… so-li.*

pepper. перца. *pyer-tsa.*

sauce. соуса. *so-u-sa.*

521. I'm sorry, it's not very good. Извините, это невкусно.
Iz-vi-ni-tye, e-ta ni-fkus-na.

522. I am not going to eat this. Я не буду это есть.
Ya ni-bu-du e-ta yest'.

523. Everything is very good. Всё очень вкусно.
Fsyo o-chin' fkus-na.

PAYING

524. What do we owe? Сколько с нас? *Skol'-ka snas?*

525. Check, please. Счёт, пожалуйста.
Schyot, pa-zha-lus-ta.

526. Everything on one bill, please.
Всё на один счёт, пожалуйста.
Fsyo na-a-din schyot, pa-zha-lus-ta.

527. Could we divide the bill in half?
Можно поделить пополам?
Mozh-na pa-di-lit' pa-pa-lam?

528. Is the tip included in the total? Чаевые включены в счёт?
Cha-yi-vî-ye fklyu-chi-nî f-schyot?

529. You counted incorrectly. Вы неправильно посчитали.
Vî ni-pra-vil'-na pa-schi-ta-li.

530. I owe less. Я должен меньше. *Ya dol-zhîn myen'-she.*

531. This is extra. Это лишнее. *E-ta lish'-ni-ye.*

532. Do I pay here or at the cash register?
Платить здесь или у кассы? *Pla-tit' zdyes' i-li u-kas-sî?*

Chapter 6
Staying in Touch

TELEPHONE CONVERSATION

533. Hello?   Алло́?   *A-lo?*

534. Who is speaking?   Кто говори́т?   *Kto ga-va-rit?*

535. Is this… Igor Vladimirovich?
Это… И́горь Влади́мирович?
E-ta… I-gar Vla-di-mi-ra-vich?

the restaurant.   рестора́н.   *ris-ta-ran.*

the box office.   биле́тные ка́ссы.
bi-lyet-ni-ye kas-si.

536. Who are you looking for?   Кто вам ну́жен?
Kto vam nu-zhin?

537. I'm looking for Mr. Petrushevsky.
Мне ну́жен господи́н Петруше́вский.
Mnye nu-zhin gas-pa-din Pi-tru-shef-skiy.

538. That's me.   Это я.   *E-ta ya.*

539. It's James speaking.   Говори́т Джеймс.
Ga-va-rit Dzheyms.

540. You've got the wrong number.   Вы не туда́ попа́ли.
Vî ni-tu-da pa-pa-li.

541. You're breaking up.   Пло́хо слы́шно.   *Plo-ha slîsh-na.*

542. Please call Masha (to the telephone).
Пожа́луйста, позови́те Ма́шу.
Pa-zha-lus-ta, pa-za-vi-tye Ma-shu.

543. He / She isn't here.   Его́ / Её нет.   *Yi-vo / Yi-yo nyet.*

544. Please tell them that Diana called.
Пожа́луйста, скажи́те, что звони́ла Диа́на.
Pa-zha-lus-ta, ska-zhî-tye, shto zva-ni-la Di-a-na.

545. I'll call back.   Я перезвоню́.   *Ya pi-ri-zva-nyu.*

546. What is your number?   Како́й ваш но́мер?
Ka-koy vash no-mir?

547. My telephone number is 514-5938.
Мой но́мер телефо́на пять оди́н четы́ре, пятьдеся́т де́вять, три́дцать во́семь.
Moy no-mir ti-li-fo-na pyat' a-din chi-tî-ri pi-di-syat dye-vit' tri-tsat' vo-sim.

MOBILE SERVICE

548. Do you have mobile phones?
У вас есть моби́льные телефо́ны?
U-vas yest' ma-bil-nî-ye ti-li-fo-nî?

549. I have a phone, I need a SIM-card.
У меня́ есть телефо́н, мне нужна́ СИМ-ка́рта.
U-mi-nya yest' ti-li-fon, mnye nuzh-na sim-kar-ta.

550. What's the rate for... calls within Moscow?
Како́й тари́ф на... звонки́ по Москве́?
Ka-koy ta-rif na... zvan-ki pa-mask-vye?

calls within Russia?   звонки́ по Росси́и?
zvan-ki pa-ra-si-i?

international calls?   зарубе́жные звонки́?
za-ru-byezh-nî-ye zvan-ki?

text messages... within Russia?   СМС... по Росси́и.
es-em-es... pa-ra-si-i?

abroad?   зарубе́ж?   *za-ru-byesh?*

551. What is the price... per minute?
Скóлько стóит... однá минýта?
Skol'-ka sto-it... ad-na mi-nu-ta?

per call?   оди́н звонóк?   *a-din zva-nok?*

552. How can I check the balance?
Как мóжно провéрить балáнс?
Kak mozh-na pra-vye-rit' ba-lans?

553. Will this card work with my phone?
Эта кáрта бýдет рабóтать с мои́м телефóном?
E-ta kar-ta bu-dit ra-bo-tat' sma-im ti-li-fo-nam?

554. This is a regular SIM-card, I need a micro-SIM.
Это обы́чная СИМ-кáрта, а мне нужнá микро-СИ́М.
E-ta a-bich-na-ya sim-kar-ta, a mnye nuzh-na mi-kra-sim.

555. How do I activate this card?   Как активи́ровать э́ту
кáрту?
Kak ak-ti-vi-ra-vat' e-tu kar-tu?

556. What is my phone number?   Какóй мой нóмер телефóна?
Ka-koy moy no-mir ti-li-fo-na?

557. What is the... country code?   Какóй...код страны́?
Ka-koy... kot stra-ni?

city code?   код гóрода?   *kot go-ra-da?*

558. Do you know the country code for... Australia?
Вы не знáете какóй код в... Австрáлии?
Vi ni-znay-tye ka-koy kot v... Af-stra-li-i?

PHONE CARDS

559. Do you have phone cards?
У вас есть телефóнные кáрточки?
U-vas yest' ti-li-fon-ni-ye kar-tach-ki?

560. Can you tell me where they have them?
Где есть, не подскáжете?
Gdye yest', ni-pat-ska-zhi-tye?

561. Please give me a phone card for... 100 rubles.
   Дайте, пожалуйста, карточку на... сто рублей.
   ***Day*-tye, pa-*zha*-lus-ta, kar-tach-ku na... sto ru-*bley*.**

   500 rubles.   пятьсот рублей.   ***pit-sot* ru-*bley*.**

   1,000.   тысячу.   ***ti*-si-chu.**

562. Can I use this card to call the U.S.?
   По этой карточке можно звонить в Америку?
   ***Pa-e*-tay kar-tach-kye *mozh*-na zva-*nit'* va-*mye*-ri-ku?**

563. Please explain how to use the card.
   Объясните, пожалуйста, как пользоваться карточкой.
   ***Ab-yis-ni*-tye, pa-*zha*-lus-ta, kak *pol'*-za-vat-sa kar-tach-kai.**

564. Excuse me, is there a payphone around here?
   Извините, где-нибудь здесь есть телефон-автомат?
   ***Iz-vi-ni*-tye, *gdye*-ni-but' zdyes' yest' ti-li-*fon* af-ta-*mat*?**

565. Operator?   Оператор?   ***A-pi-ra*-tar?**

566. I'm trying to make a call with a phonecard.
   Я пытаюсь позвонить по карточке.
   ***Ya pi-ta*-yus' pa-zva-*nit'* pa-*kar*-tach-kye.**

567. What is your card number?
   Какой номер вашей карточки?
   ***Ka-koy no*-mir *va*-shiy *kar*-tach-ki?**

568. What number are you calling?
   По какому номеру вы звоните?
   ***Pa-ka-ko*-mu *no*-mi-ru vi zva-*ni*-tye?**

POST OFFICE

569. Excuse me, where is the post office?
   Извините, вы не знаете где почта?
   ***Iz-vi-ni*-tye, *vi* ni-*znay*-tye gdye *poch*-ta?**

570. I need to mail a… postcard.
Мне нýжно отпрáвить… откры́тку.
Mnye nuzh-na at-pra-vit' at-krit-ku.

letter. письмó. *pis'-mo.*

package. посы́лку. *pa-sil-ku.*

571. Where to? Кудá? *Ku-da?*

572. To… Moscow. В… Москвý. *V… Mask-vu.*

St. Petersburg. Пи́тер. *Pi-tir.*

the U.S. Амéрику. *A-mye-ri-ku.*

Canada. Канáду. *Ka-na-du.*

573. What type of mail do you need?
Какóй вид пóчты вам нýжен?
Ka-koy vit poch-ti vam nu-zhin?

574. Regular. Обы́чная. *A-bich-na-ya.*

Registered. Заказнáя. *Za-kaz-na-ya.*

Express. Экспрéсс. *Eks-press.*

575. How long will it take (to arrive)? Как дóлго бýдет идти́?
Kak dol-ga bu-dit i-ti?

576. Where do I write the address? Где писáть áдрес?
Gdye pi-sat' ad-res?

577. Can I write in English? Мóжно писáть по-англи́йски?
Mozh-na pi-sat' pa-an-gli-ski?

578. I need… envelopes. Мне нужны́… конвéрты.
Mnye nuzh-ni… kan-vyer-ti.

stamps. мáрки. *mar-ki.*

boxes. корóбки. *ka-rop-ki.*

579. Can you send a fax? Вы мóжете отпрáвить факс?
Vi mo-zhi-tye at-pra-vit' faks?

580. How many pages? Скóлько страни́ц?
Skol'-ka stra-nits?

581. One page.   Одна́ страни́ца.   *Ad-na stra-ni-tsa.*

Two pages.   Две страни́цы.   *Dvye stra-ni-tsî.*

Five pages.   Пять страни́ц.   *Pyat' stra-nits.*

INTERNET AND COMPUTERS

582. I need to get online.   Мне ну́жно вы́йти в сеть.
Mnye nuzh-na viy-ti fsyet'.

583. I want to check my mail (email).
Я хочу́ прове́рить по́чту (име́йл).
Ya ha-chu pra-vye-rit' poch-tu (i-meyl).

584. Excuse me, I am looking for an Internet café.
Извини́те, я ищу́ интерне́т кафе́.
Iz-vi-ni-tye, ya i-schu in-ter-net ka-fe.

585. Is there a "hot-spot" (wi-fi) here?
Здесь есть хот-спо́т (вай-фа́й)?
Zdyes' yest' hot-spot (vay-fay)?

586. I have my own… laptop.   У меня́ свой… лапто́п.
U-mi-nya svoy… lap-top.

smartphone.   смартфо́н.   *smart-fon.*

tablet.   планше́т.   *plan-shet.*

587. Is there an electric outlet here?
Здесь есть розе́тка?
Zdyes' yest' ra-zyet-ka?

588. Help me connect to the Internet.
Помоги́те мне подключи́ться к Интерне́ту.
Pa-ma-gi-tye mnye pat-klyu-chit-sa kIn-ter-ne-tu.

589. What is your network called?
Как называ́ется ва́ша сеть?
Kak na-zî-va-it-sa va-sha syet'?

590. What is the password?   Како́й паро́ль?
Ka-koy pa-rol'?

591. Please write it down.   Запишите, пожалуйста.
Za-pi-shî-tye, pa-zha-lus-ta.

592. I can't connect.   Я не могу соединиться.
Ya ni-ma-gu say-di-nit-sa.

593. Is your Internet working?   Ваш Интернет работает?
Vash in-ter-net ra-bo-ta-it?

594. I'm connected.   Я соединился.   **Ya say-di-nil-sa.**

595. It's not working.   Не работает.   **Ni-ra-bo-ta-it.**

596. It's working, but very slowly.
Работает, но очень медленно.
Ra-bo-ta-it, no o-chin' myed-li-na.

597. What's the web browser here?   Какой здесь браузер?
Ka-koy zdyes' bra-u-zer?

598. Is there… Skype here?   Здесь есть… Скайп?
Zdyes' yest' Skayp?

    Word.   Ворд.   **Vort.**

    Photoshop.   Фотошоп.   **Fo-ta-shop.**

    iTunes.   Айтюнс.   **Ay-tyuns.**

    PowerPoint.   ПауерПоинт.   **pa-u-er-poynt.**

    a word processor.   текстовый процессор.
    tyek-sta-vîy pra-tse-sar.

    an ftp-client.   фтп-клиент.   **ef-te-pe kli-yent.**

    a BitTorrent-client.   битторрент-клиент.
    bit-tor-rent kli-yent.

599. Do you have… headphones (with a microphone)?
У вас есть… наушники (с микрофоном)?
U-vas yest'… na-ush-ni-ki (smi-kra-fo-nam)?

    printer.   принтер.   **prin-ter.**

    blank disks.   чистые диски.   **chis-tî-ye dis-ki.**

600. Can this drive record to (burn) a DVD?
Этот драйв может записать ДВД?
E-tat drayf mo-zhît za-pi-sat' de-ve-de?

601. I'd like to print a document.
Я хочу́ распеча́тать докуме́нт.
Ya ha-<u>chu</u> ras-pi-<u>cha</u>-tat' da-ku-<u>myent</u>.

602. Is the printer color or black-and-white?
При́нтер цветно́й и́ли черно-бе́лый?
<u>Prin</u>-ter tsvit-<u>noy</u> i-li chir-na-<u>bye</u>-liy?

603. My flash drive …is not mounting.
Моя́ флэ́шка …не чита́ется.
Ma-<u>ya</u> <u>flesh</u>-ka …ni-chi-<u>ta</u>-it-sa.

My (external) drive.   Мой драйв.   *Moy drayf.*

604. This is a PC, and I need a Mac.
Это ПиСи́, а мне ну́жен Мак.
<u>E</u>-ta Pi-Si, a mnye <u>nu</u>-zhin mak.

Chapter 7
Culture and Entertainment

WHERE TO GO?

605. Where should we go (this evening)?
Куда́ нам пойти́ (сего́дня ве́чером)?
Ku-da nam pay-ti (si-vod-nya vye-chi-ram)?

606. To a... museum.   В... музе́й.   *V... mu-zyey.*

   gallery.   галлере́ю.   *ga-li-rye-yu.*

   theater.   ти-atr.   *meátp.*

   movie.   кино́.   *ki-no.*

   club.   клуб.   *klup.*

   park.   парк.   *park.*

   swimming pool.   бассе́йн.   *ba-seyn.*

607. To a... sports event.   На... стадио́н.   *Na... sta-di-on.*

   ballet.   бале́т.   *ba-leyt.*

   concert.   конце́рт.   *kan-tsert.*

   play.   спекта́кль.   *spik-takl'.*

   beach.   пляж.   *plyash.*

   party.   вечери́нку.   *vi-chi-rin-ku.*

608. Are there any interesting... plays?
Каки́е есть интере́сные... спекта́кли?
Ka-ki-ye yest' in-ti-ryes-nî-ye... spik-tak-li?

   films.   фи́льмы.   *fil'-mî.*

   concerts.   конце́рты.   *kan-tser-tî.*

609. We want to see churches and monasteries.
Мы хоти́м посмотре́ть це́ркви и монастыри́.
Mî ha-tim pas-mat-ryet' tserk-vi i-ma-nas-tî-ri.

610. I want to go on a walking tour.
Я хочу́ пойти́ на экску́рсию по го́роду.
Ya ha-chu pay-ti na-eks-kur-si-yu pa-go-ra-du.

611. I'm interested in architecture.
Меня́ интересу́ет архитекту́ра.
Mi-nya in-ti-ri-su-it ar-hi-tik-tu-ra.

612. What are you interested in?   Что вас интересу́ет?
Shto vas in-ti-ri-su-it?

613. Contemporary art and dance.
Совреме́нное иску́сство и та́нец.
Sav-ri-myen-na-ye is-kust-va i-ta-nits.

614. And in music?   А му́зыка?   *A-mu-zî-ka?*

615. Jazz.   Джаз.   *Dzhaz.*
rock.   рок.   *rok.*
blues.   блюз.   *blyuz.*
electronica.   электро́ника.   *e-lik-tro-ni-ka.*
any music.   люба́я му́зыка.   *lyu-ba-ya mu-zî-ka.*

616. This venue has only classical music.
В э́том за́ле то́лько класси́ческая му́зыка.
Ve-tam za-lye tol'-ka kla-si-chis-ka-ya mu-zî-ka.

617. Is there a bar with live music?
Есть како́й-нибудь бар с живо́й му́зыкой?
Yest' ka-koy-ni-but' bar zzhî-voy mu-zî-kay?

618. What sports do you like?   Како́й спорт вы лю́бите?
Ka-koy sport vî lyu-bi-tye?

619. Soccer, basketball, volleyball, hockey.
Футбо́л, баскетбо́л, волейбо́л, хокке́й.
Fud-bol, bas-kid-bol, va-liy-bol, ha-kyey.

620. What teams do you have here? Какие здесь команды?
Ka-_ki_-ye zdyes' ka-_man_-dî?

621. What do you recommend? Что вы рекомендуете?
Shto vî ri-ka-min-_duy_-tye?

622. What's playing... today? Что идёт... сегодня?
Shto i-_dyot_... si-_vod_-nya?

tomorrow. завтра. **_zaf_-tra.**

the day after tomorrow. послезавтра. **pos-li-_zaf_-tra.**

over the weekend. на выходных. **na-vî-had-_nîh_.**

623. What's at the... Bolshoi? Что... в Большом?
Shto... vBal'-_shom_?

Pioneer cinema. в кинотеатре Пионер.
fki-na-_tyat_-rye Pi-a-_nyer_.

Moscow Art Theater. во МХАТе. **va _Mha_-tye.**

624. Who's... playing? Кто... играет? **Kto... i-_gra_-it?**

singing. поёт. **pa-_yot_.**

performing. выступает. **vîs-tu-_pa_-it.**

dancing. танцует. **tan-_tsu_-it.**

conducting. дирижёр. **di-ri-_zhor_.**

625. Who's the director? Кто режиссёр? **Kto ri-zhî-_syor_?**

626. Who's in the leading role? Кто в главной роли?
Kto _vglav_-nay _ro_-li?

627. When does it start? Когда начало?
Kag-_da_ na-_cha_-la?

628. How much is a ticket? Сколько стоит билет?
Skol'-ka _sto_-it bi-_lyet_?

TICKETS AND RESERVATIONS

629. I'd like to order tickets for the... play.
Я хочу́ заказа́ть биле́ты на... спекта́кль.
*Ya ha-**chu** za-ka-**zat'** bi-**lye**-tî na-... spik-**takl'**.*

opera.   о́перу.   ***o**-pi-ru.*

concert.   конце́рт.   *kan-**tsert**.*

630. Today everything is sold out.   Сего́дня всё распро́дано.
*Si-**vod**-nya fsyo ras-**pro**-da-na.*

631. There are no tickets (left).   Биле́тов нет.
*Bi-**lye**-taf nyet.*

632. Do you have tickets for... tomorrow?
Есть биле́ты на... за́втра?
*Yest' bi-**lye**-tî na-... **zaf**-tra?*

the next showing.   сле́дующий сеа́нс.
***slye**-du-schiy si-**ans**.*

633. How many do you need?   Ско́лько вам ну́жно?
***Skol**'-ka vam **nuzh**-na?*

634. I need three tickets... in the orchestra.
Мне ну́жно три биле́та... в парте́ре.
*Mnye **nuzh**-na tri bi-**lye**-ta... fpar-**te**-rye.*

in the mezzanine.   в бельэта́же.   *vbi-lye-**ta**-zhe.*

in a box.   в ло́же.   *v**lo**-zhe.*

at the center.   в середи́не за́ла.   *fsi-ri-**di**-nye **za**-la.*

close to the stage.   побли́же к сце́не.
*pa-**bli**-zhe k **stse**-nye.*

in the first row.   в пе́рвом ряду́.   *f**pyer**-vam rya-**du**.*

not too pricey.   не о́чень дороги́х.
*ni-**o**-chin' da-ra-**gih**.*

635. How much is it all together?   Ско́лько всё вме́сте?
***Skol**'-ka fsyo **vmyes**-tye?*

636. I'll pay with a credit card.   Я заплачу́ ка́рточкой.
*Ya za-pla-**chu kar**-tach-kay.*

637. We take only cash. Здесь то́лько нали́чными.
Zdyes' tol'-ka na-lich-ni-mi.

638. Can I pay at the box office? Мо́жно заплати́ть в ка́ссе?
Mozh-na za-pla-tit' fkas-sye?

639. Where can I pick up the tickets?
Где мо́жно забра́ть биле́ты?
Gdye mozh-na za-brat' bi-lye-ti?

640. Do we pick up our tickets at the box office?
Биле́ты забира́ть в ка́ссе?
Bi-lye-ti za-bi-rat' fkas-sye?

641. When does... the box office open?
Когда́ открыва́ется... ка́сса?
Kag-da ot-krî-va-yit-sa... kas-sa?

museum. музе́й. *mu-zyey.*

the gallery. галлере́я. *ga-li-rye-ya.*

the theater. теа́тр. *ti-atr.*

THEATER, MOVIES

642. When does the... play begin?
Когда́ начина́ется... спекта́кль?
Kag-da na-chi-na-yit-sa... spik-takl'?

643. How long is... the film? Ско́лько идёт... фильм?
Skol'-ka i-dyot... fil'm?

644. Is the film... dubbed? Фильм... дубли́рован?
Fil'm... dub-li-ra-van?

subtitled. с субти́трами. *ssup-ti-tra-mi.*

645. Tickets, please. Биле́ты, пожа́луйста.
Bi-lye-ti pa-zha-lus-ta.

646. Here are our tickets. Вот на́ши биле́ты.
Vot na-shî bi-lye-ti.

647. Excuse me, are these seats taken?
Извини́те, э́ти места́ за́няты?
Iz-vi-ni-tye, e-ti mis-ta za-ni-ti?

648. Excuse me, these are our seats.
Извини́те, э́то на́ши места́.
Iz-vi-<u>ni</u>-tye, <u>e</u>-ta <u>na</u>-shî mis-<u>ta</u>.

649. Is there an intermission?   Бу́дет антра́кт?
<u>Bu</u>-dit ant-<u>rakt</u>?

650. Where is the... bar?   Где... бар?   *Gdye... bar?*

snack bar.   буфе́т.   *bu-<u>fyet</u>.*

bathroom.   туале́ты.   *tu-a-<u>lye</u>-tî.*

coat check.   гардеро́б.   *gar-di-<u>rop</u>.*

MUSEUM

651. What exhibitions are now on view at the museum?
Каки́е вы́ставки сейча́с в музе́е?
Ka-<u>ki</u>-ye <u>vîs</u>-taf-ki siy-<u>chas</u> vmu-<u>zye</u>-ye?

652. What is the entry fee?   Ско́лько сто́ит вход?
<u>Skol'</u>-ka <u>sto</u>-it fhot?

653. (Today) entry is free.   (Сего́дня) вход беспла́тный.
(Si-<u>vod</u>-nya) vhot bis-<u>plat</u>-nîy.

654. Is there a discount for... students?
Есть ски́дка для... студе́нтов?
Yest' <u>skit</u>-ka dlya... stu-<u>dyen</u>-taf?

seniors.   пожилы́х.   *pa-zhî-<u>lîh</u>.*

children.   дете́й.   *di-<u>tyey</u>.*

655. Do you have... a map of the museum (in English)?
У вас есть... план музе́я (на англи́йском)?
U-vas yest'... plan mu-<u>zye</u>-ya (na-an-<u>glis</u>-kam)?

an audio guide.   а́удио-гид.   *a-u-di-a-<u>git</u>.*

guided tours.   экску́рсии.   *eks-<u>kur</u>-si-i.*

656. In what language?   На како́м языке́?
Na-ka-<u>kom</u> yi-zî-<u>kye</u>?

657. When is the next tour (in English)?
Когда́ сле́дующая экску́рсия (на англи́йском)?
Kag-da slye-duy-scha-ya eks-kur-si-ya (na-an-glis-kam)?

658. How long is the tour?   Ско́лько дли́тся экску́рсия?
Skol'-ka dlit-sa eks-kur-si-ya?

659. Can we hire a private guide?   Мы мо́жем наня́ть ги́да?
Mî mo-zhîm na-nyat' gi-da?

660. Does the guide speak English?
Гид говори́т по-англи́йски?
Git ga-va-rit pa-an-gli-ski?

661. Excuse me, who is the... painter?
Извини́те, кто... худо́жник?
Iz-vi-ni-tye, kto... hu-dozh-nik?

   sculptor.   ску́льптор.   *skul'p-tar.*

   photographer.   фото́граф.   *fa-tog-raf.*

662. What is the name of this piece?
Как называ́ется э́та рабо́та?
Kak na-zî-va-it-sa e-ta ra-bo-ta?

663. Where are the galleries of... contemporary art?
Где галере́и... совреме́нного иску́сства?
Gdye ga-li-rye-i... sav-ri-myen-na-va is-kust-va?

   ancient art.   дре́внего иску́сства.
   dryev-ni-va is-kust-va.

   Russian art.   ру́сского иску́сства.
   rus-ka-va is-kust-va.

   classical sculpture.   класси́ческой скульпту́ры.
   kla-si-chis-kay skul'p-tu-rî.

   Renaissance art.   иску́сства ренесса́нса.
   is-kust-va ri-ni-san-sa.

   modernism.   модерни́зма.   *ma-der-niz-ma.*

   photography.   фотогра́фии.   *fa-ta-gra-fi-i.*

   Soviet art.   сове́тского иску́сства.
   sa-vyet-ska-va is-kust-va.

ART GALLERY

664. Is this for sale?   Это продаётся?   *E-ta pra-da-yot-sa?*

665. Do you have any information on the artist (in English)?
У вас есть информа́ция о худо́жнике (на англи́йском)?
*U-vas yest' in-far-ma-tsî-ya a-hu-dozh-ni-kye
(na-an-glis-kam)?*

666. Can I get in touch with the artist?
Мо́жно связа́ться с худо́жником?
Mozh-na svi-zat-sa s hu-dozh-ni-kam?

667. When was this work painted?
Когда́ была́ напи́сана э́та рабо́та?
Kag-da bî-la na-pi-sa-na e-ta ra-bo-ta?

668. From what year is this piece?   Како́го го́да эта рабо́та?
Ka-ko-va go-da e-ta ra-bo-ta?

669. When does this show close?
Когда́ закрыва́ется вы́ставка?
Kag-da za-krî-va-yit-sa vîs-taf-ka?

670. Do you have a catalog of... this show?
У вас есть катало́г... э́той вы́ставки?
U-vas yest' ka-ta-lok... e-tay vîs-taf-ki?

the previous show.   предыду́щей вы́ставки.
pri-dî-du-schiy vîs-taf-ki.

671. Will I be able to take this work out of the country?
Я смогу́ вы́везти э́ту рабо́ту заграни́цу?
Ya sma-gu vî-vis-ti e-tu ra-bo-tu za-gra-ni-tsu?

SIGHTSEEING

672. When was this built?   Когда́ э́то стро́или?
Kag-da e-ta stro-i-li?

673. Who is the architect?   Кто архите́ктор?
Kto ar-hi-tyek-tar?

674. Is this a restoration?   Э́то реставра́ция?
E-ta ris-tav-ra-tsî-ya?

675. What was here… earlier?   Что здесь бы́ло… ра́ньше?
Shto zdyes' bî-la… ran'-she?

during Soviet rule.   при сове́тской вла́сти.
pri-sa-vyets-kay vlas-ti.

before Soviet rule.   до сове́тской вла́сти.
da-sa-vyets-kay vlas-ti.

676. What is this place now?   Что здесь сейча́с?
Shto zdyes' siy-chas?

677. Is it a functioning… church?
Э́то де́йствующая… це́рковь?
E-ta dyey-stvu-yu-scha-ya… tser-kaf?

mosque.   мече́ть.   *mi-chyet'.*

synagogue.   синаго́га.   *si-na-go-ga.*

678. Can I take photographs here?
Здесь мо́жно фотографи́ровать?
Zdyes' mozh-na fa-ta-gra-fi-ra-vat'?

679. Could you take a photo of us / me?
Вы мо́жете сфотографи́ровать нас / меня́?
Vî mo-zhî-tye sfa-ta-gra-fi-ra-vat' nas / mi-nya?

SPORTS AND LEISURE

680. Do you play any sports?   Вы занима́етесь спо́ртом?
Vî za-ni-may-tyes' spor-tam?

681. I do swim and dive.   Я пла́ваю и ныря́ю.
Ya pla-va-yu i-nî-rya-yu.

682. I… bike.   Я ката́юсь на… велосипе́де.
Ya ka-ta-yus' na… vi-la-si-pye-dye.

(water)ski.   (во́дных) лы́жах.   *(vod-nîh) lî-zhah.*

ice skate   конька́х.   *kan'-kah.*

683. I play... hockey.   Я игра́ю... в хокке́й.
Ya i-_gra_-yu... fha-_kyey_.

golf.   в гольф.   **_vgol'f_.**

basketball.   в баскетбо́л.   **_vbas_-kid-_bol_.**

684. Would you like to play a game of... tennis?
Хоти́те сыгра́ть... в те́ннис?
Ha-_ti_-tye sîg-_rat'_... _fte_-nis?

ping-pong.   в пинг-по́нг.   **_fping-ponk_.**

chess.   в ша́хматы.   **_fshah_-ma-tî.**

685. Where can I rent... a bicycle?
Где мо́жно взять напрока́т... велосипе́д?
Gdye _mozh_-na vzyat' na-pra-_kat_... vi-la-si-_pyet_?

skis.   лы́жи.   **_lî-zhî_.**

skates.   коньки́.   **kan'-_ki_.**

a boat.   ло́дку.   **_lot_-ku.**

686. I need... a bathing suit.   Мне ну́жен... купа́льник.
Mnye _nu_-zhîn... ku-_pal'_-nik.

a lock.   замо́к.   **za-_mok_.**

(need) a swimming cap.   нужна́ ша́почка для пла́вания.
nuzh-_na sha_-pach-ka dlya _pla_-va-nya.

snorkel.   тру́бка.   **_trup_-ka.**

(need) swimming goggles.   нужны́ очки́ (для пла́ванья).
nuzh-_nî_ ach-_ki_ (dlya _pla_-va-nya).

flippers.   ла́сты.   **_las_-tî.**

ear plugs.   заты́чки для уше́й.   **za-_tîch_-ki dlya u-_shey_.**

(need) a towel.   ну́жно полоте́нце.
nuzh-na pa-la-_tyen_-tse.

687. Where can I... swim around here?
Где здесь мо́жно... искупа́ться?
Gdye zdyes' _mozh_-na... is-ku-_pat_-sa?

play tennis.   сыгра́ть... в те́ннис.   **sîg-_rat'_... _fte_-nis.**

play billiards.   в биллиа́рд.   **_vbil-yard_.**

688. I'd rather watch than play.
Я не люблю́ игра́ть, я люблю́ смотре́ть.
Ya ni-lyub-lyu ig-rat', ya lyub-lyu sma-tryet'.

689. What's the score?   Како́й счёт?   *Ka-koy schot?*

HIKING AND CAMPING

690. We want to go camping.   Мы хоти́м пойти́ в похо́д.
Mî ha-tim pay-ti fpa-hot.

691. I want to go on a trip... out of town.
Я хочу́ пое́хать на экску́рсию... за́ город.
Ya ha-chu pa-ye-hat' na-eks-kur-si-yu... za-ga-rat.

into the mountains.   в го́ры.   *vgo-rî.*

to Lake Baikal.   на Байка́л.   *na-Bay-kal.*

to the south.   на юг.   *na-yuk.*

692. How do we get there?   Как туда́ попа́сть?
Kak tu-da pa-past'?

693. Can we get there... by car?
Туда́ мо́жно дое́хать... на маши́не?
Tu-da mozh-na da-ye-hat'... na-ma-shi-nye?

train.   по́ездом.   *po-yiz-dam.*

694. Can we camp there?
Там мо́жно поста́вить пала́тку?
Tam mozh-na pa-sta-vit' pa-lat-ku?

695. Where can we rent a tent?
Где мо́жно взять напрока́т пала́тку?
Gdye mozh-na vzyat' na-pra-kat pa-lat-ku?

696. Is there a campground there?   Там есть ка́мпинг?
Tam yest' kam-ping?

697. Can we leave our car here?
Здесь мо́жно оста́вить маши́ну?
Zdyes' mozh-na as-ta-vit' ma-shi-nu?

698. What is the name of... this place?
Как называется...это место?
Kak na-zi-va-it-sa... e-ta myes-ta?

this mountain.   эта гора.   *e-ta ga-ra.*

this forest.   этот лес.   *e-tat lyes.*

this lake.   это озеро.   *e-ta o-zi-ra.*

699. Where does this road lead to?   Куда ведёт эта дорога?
Ku-da vi-dyot e-ta da-ro-ga?

700. Where is the bridge to cross the river?
Где мост через реку?
Gdye most che-ris rye-ku?

701. Can you tell me how to get back to... the main road?
Вы не знаете, как вернуться... на главную дорогу?
Vi ni-znay-tye, kak vir-nut-sa... na-glav-nu-yu da-ro-gu?

the trailhead.   к началу тропы.   *kna-cha-lu tro-pî.*

the parking lot.   к стоянке.   *ksta-yan-kye.*

702. Excuse me, where is... the nearest town?
Извините, где... ближайший город?
Iz-vi-ni-tye, gdye... bli-zhay-shîy go-rat?

nearest village.   ближайшая деревня.
bli-zhay-sha-ya di-ryev-nya.

station.   станция.   *stan-tsî-ya.*

703. We are out of... water.   У нас нет... воды.
U-nas nyet... va-dî.

food.   еды.   *yi-dî*

gasoline.   бензина.   *bin-zi-na.*

matches.   спичек.   *spi-chik.*

704. My phone is dead.   Мой телефон разрядился.
Moy ti-li-fon raz-ri-dil-sa.

705. Please let us use your phone.
Пожалуйста, одолжите ваш телефон.
Pa-zha-lus-ta, a-dal-zhî-tye vash ti-li-fon.

706. Where can we find...   Где мо́жно найти́...
     Gdye _mozh_-na nay-_ti_...

707. Where are we?   Где мы?   **Gdye mî?**

708. We are lost.   Мы заблуди́лись.   **Mî za-blu-_di_-lis'.**

709. Our... tent has been stolen.   У нас укра́ли... пала́тку.
     U-nas u-_kra_-li... pa-_lat_-ku.

     car.   маши́ну.   **ma-_shi_-nu.**

     gasoline.   бензи́н.   **bin-_zin_.**

     backpack.   рюкза́к.   **ryug-_zak_.**

710. I was bitten by a snake.   Меня́ укуси́ла змея́.
     Mi-_nya_ u-ku-_si_-la zmi-_ya_.

711. Please help!   Помоги́те, пожа́луйста.
     Pa-ma-_gi_-tye, pa-_zha_-lus-ta.

Chapter 8
Health and Safety

ILLNESS AND MEDICAL EMERGENCIES

712. What's wrong?   Что с вáми?   *Shto sva-mi?*

713. I'm not well.   Мне плóхо.   *Mnye plo-ha.*

714. I am ill. *(m./f.)*   Я бóлен / больнá.   *Ya bo-lin / bal'-na.*

715. Help!   Помогúте!   *Pa-ma-gi-tye!*

716. What happened?   Что случúлось?   *Shto slu-chi-las'?*

717. I fell. *(m./f.)*   Я упáл(а).   *Ya u-pal(-a).*

718. I lost consciousness. *(m./f.)*   Я потерял(а) сознáние.
Ya pa-ti-ryal(-a) sa-zna-nye.

719. I was hit by a car.   Меня сбúла машúна.
Mi-nya zbi-la ma-shî-na.

720. I can't feel my… arm (hand).   Я не чýвствую рýку.
Ya ni-chust-vu-yu… ru-ku.

   leg (foot).   нóгу.   *no-gu.*

721. I'm nauseous.   Меня тошнúт.   *Mi-nya tash-nit.*

722. I have food poisoning. *(m./f.)*   Я отравúлся / отравúлась.
Ya at-ra-vil-sa / ot-ra-vi-las'.

723. I'm dizzy.   У меня крýжится головá.
U-mi-nya kru-zhît-sa ga-la-va.

724. I need a doctor.   Мне нýжно к врачý.
    Mnye __nuzh__-na kvra-__chu__.

725. I need to get to a hospital.   Мне нýжно в больнúцу.
    Mnye __nuzh__-na vbal'-__ni__-tsu.

726. Please call a doctor.   Пожáлуйста, позовúте врачá.
    Pa-__zha__-lus-ta, pa-za-__vi__-tye vra-__cha__.

727. Call an ambulance.   Вы́зовите скóрую пóмощь.
    __Vi__-za-vi-tye __sko__-ru-yu __po__-masch.

728. Don't worry.   Не беспокóйтесь.   *Ni-bis-pa-__koy__-tis'.*

729. I'm feeling better.   Мне ужé лýчше.
    Mnye u-__zhe__ __luch__-she.

VISITING A DOCTOR OR HOSPITAL

730. Where does it hurt?   Что у вас болúт?
    Shto u-__vas__ ba-__lit__?

731. My... head hurts.   У меня́ болúт... головá.
    U-mi-__nya__ ba-__lit__... ga-la-__va__.

    throat.   гóрло.   *__gor__-la.*

    stomach.   живóт.   *zhî-__vot__.*

    arm.   рукá.   *ru-__ka__.*

732. It hurts here.   Болúт вот здесь.   *Ba-__lit__ vot zdyes'.*

733. I have... a runny nose.   У меня́... нáсморк.
    U-mi-__nya__... __nas__-mark.

    cough.   кáшель.   *__ka__-shîl'.*

    cold.   простýда.   *pras-__tu__-da.*

    fever.   температýра.   *tim-pi-ra-__tu__-ra.*

    upset stomach.   расстрóен желýдок.
    ras-__stro__-yin zhî-__lu__-dak.

    constipation.   запóр.   *za-__por__.*

    insomnia.   бессóнница.   *bis-__so__-ni-tsa.*

734. I think I broke my… arm.　　Ка́жется я слома́л… ру́ку.
Ka-zhît-sa ya sla-<u>mal</u>… <u>ru</u>-ku.

　leg.　но́гу.　*<u>no</u>-gu.*

　finger.　па́лец.　*<u>pa</u>-lits.*

　rib.　ребро́.　*rib-<u>ro</u>.*

　tooth.　зуб.　*zup.*

735. I hit my head. *(m./f.)*　　Я уши́б /уши́бла го́лову.
Ya u-<u>shîp</u> /u-shî-bla <u>go</u>-la-vu.

736. I cut myself. *(m./f.)*　　Я поре́зался / поре́залась.
Ya pa-<u>rye</u>-zal-sa / pa-<u>rye</u>-za-las'.

737. I burned myself. *(m./f.)*　　Я обжёгся / обожгла́сь.
Ya ab-<u>zhok</u>-sya / a-bazh-<u>glas</u>'.

738. I was bitten by a dog.　　Меня укуси́ла соба́ка.
Mi-<u>nya</u> u-ku-<u>si</u>-la sa-<u>ba</u>-ka.

739. I need medication.　　Мне ну́жно лека́рство.
Mnye <u>nuzh</u>-na li-<u>karst</u>-va.

740. I take… medication.　　Я принима́ю… лека́рство.
Ya pri-ni-<u>ma</u>-yu… li-<u>karst</u>-va.

　antibiotics.　антибио́тики.　*an-ti-bi-<u>o</u>-ti-ki.*

　antidepressants.　антидепресса́нты.
an-ti-di-pri-<u>san</u>-tî.

　insulin.　инсули́н　*in-su-<u>lin</u>.*

741. I am allergic to… penicillin.
У меня́ аллерги́я на… пеницилли́н.
U-mi-<u>nya</u> a-lir-gi-ya na… pi-ni-tsî-<u>lin</u>.

742. I have… heart problems.　　У меня́… больно́е се́рдце.
U-mi-<u>nya</u>… bal'-<u>no</u>-ye <u>syer</u>-tse.

　a liver problem.　больна́я пе́чень.
bal'-<u>na</u>-ya <u>pye</u>-chin'.

　stomach problems.　больно́й желу́док.
bal'-<u>noy</u> zhî-<u>lu</u>-dak.

　kidney problems.　больны́е по́чки.　*bal'-<u>nî</u>-ye <u>poch</u>-ki.*

high blood pressure.   высо́кое давле́ние.
vî-so-ka-ye dav-lye-nye.

743. I have… the flu.   У меня́… грипп.   ***U-mi-nya… grip.***

asthma.   а́стма.   ***as-ma.***

cancer.   рак.   ***rak.***

diabetes.   диабе́т.   ***di-a-bet.***

epilepsy.   эпиле́псия.   ***e-pi-lyep-si-ya.***

HIV.   ВИЧ.   ***Vich.***

744. I don't have any illnesses.   У меня́ нет никаки́х боле́зней.
U-mi-nya nyet ni-ka-kih ba-lyez-niy.

745. I'm healthy. *(m./f.)*   Я здоро́в / здоро́ва.
Ya zda-rof / zda-ro-va.

746. I need… eyeglasses.   Мне нужны́… очки́.
Mnye nuzh-nî… ach-ki.

contact lenses.   конта́ктные ли́нзы.
kan-takt-nî-ye lin-zî.

747. I need to take a… blood test.
Мне ну́жно сдать… ана́лиз кро́ви.
Mnye nuzh-na zdat'… a-na-lis kro-vi.

urine test.   ана́лиз мочи́.   ***a-na-lis ma-chi.***

748. I have all the vaccinations.   У меня́ все приви́вки.
U-mi-nya fsye pri-vif-ki.

749. I haven't been vaccinated against… hepatitis.
У меня́ нет приви́вки от… гепати́та.
U-mi-nya nyet pri-vif-ki at… gi-pa-ti-ta.

tetanus.   столбняка́.   ***stalb-ni-ka.***

tuberculosis.   туберкулёза.   ***tu-bir-ku-lyo-za.***

polio.   полиомели́та.   ***pa-lyey-mi-li-ta.***

the flu.   гри́ппа.   ***gri-pa.***

750. I (don't) smoke.   Я (не) курю́.   ***Ya (ni-) ku-ryu.***

751. I drink… moderately.　　Я пью… немно́го.
Ya pyu… ni-_mno_-ga.

a lot.　　мно́го.　　**_mno_-ga.**

752. I don't drink.　　Я не пью.　　**Ya ni-_pyu_.**

753. I (don't) use drugs.　　Я (не) по́льзуюсь нарко́тиками.
Ya (ni-) _pol_'-zu-yus' nar-_ko_-ti-ka-mi.

754. My blood type is… first (O), positive / negative.
Моя́ гру́ппа кро́ви… пе́рвая, положи́тельная /
отрица́тельная.
**Ma-_ya_ _gru_-pa _kro_-vi… _pyer_-va-ya, pa-la-_zhî_-til'-na-ya /
a-tri-_tsa_-til'-na-ya.**

second (A).　　втора́я.　　**fta-_ra_-ya.**

third (B).　　тре́тья.　　**_tryet_'-ya.**

fourth (AB).　　четвёртая.　　**chit-_vyor_-ta-ya.**

SEXUAL HEALTH

755. I am (not) pregnant.　　Я (не) бере́менна.
Ya (ni-) bi-_rye_-mi-na.

756. I'm in my… third month.　　Я на… тре́тьем месяце.
Ya na… _trye_-tim _mye_-si-tse.

fifth.　　пя́том.　　**_pya_-tam.**

eighth.　　восьмо́м.　　**vas'-_mom_.**

757. I'm (not) sexually active. I have… one partner.
Я (не) занима́юсь се́ксом. У меня́… оди́н партнёр.
Ya (ni-) za-ni-_ma_-yus' _sek_-sam. U me-_nya_… a-_din_ part-_nyor_.

multiple partners.　　не́сколько партнёров.
nye-skal'-ka part-_nyo_-raf.

758. I am taking birth control.
Я принима́ю противозача́точные табле́тки.
Ya pri-ni-_ma_-yu pra-ti-va-za-_cha_-tach-nî-ye tab-_lyet_-ki.

759. I am having (ir)regular periods.
У меня́ (не)норма́льная менструа́ция.
U-mi-__nya__ (ni-) nar-__mal__'-na-ya min-stru-__a__-tsî-ya.

760. I have a... urinary tract infection.
У меня́... воспале́ние мочево́го кана́ла.
U-mi-__nya__... vas-pa-__lye__-nye ma-chi-__vo__-va ka-__na__-la.

761. I had unprotected sex. *(m./f.)*
Я занима́лся / занима́лась се́ксом без защи́ты.
Ya za-ni-__mal__-sa / za-ni-__ma__-las' __syek__-sam biz-za-__schi__-tî.

762. I need to take a test for... HIV.
Мне ну́жно сде́лать ана́лиз на... ВИЧ.
Mnye __nuzh__-na __zdye__-lat' a-__na__-lis na... Vich.

venereal disease (STDs).
венери́ческие заболева́ния.
vi-ni-__ri__-chis-ki-ye za-ba-li-__va__-nya.

pregnancy.   бере́менность.   *bi-__rye__-mi-nast'.*

763. When can I have the results?
Когда́ мо́жно бу́дет получи́ть результа́т?
Kag-__da__ __mozh__-na __bu__-dit pa-lu-__chit__' ri-zul'-__tat__?

AGREEING TO AND PAYING FOR MEDICAL SERVICES

764. Yes, I agree. *(m./f.)*   Да, я согла́сен / согла́сна.
Da, ya sag-__la__-sin / sag-__las__-na.

765. No, I do not agree. *(m./f.)*   Нет, я не согла́сен / согла́сна.
Nyet, ya ni-sag-__la__-sin / ni-sag-__las__-na.

766. I (don't) need an operation.   Мне (не) нужна́ опера́ция.
Mnye (ni-) nuzh-__na__ a-pi-__ra__-tsî-ya.

767. I (don't) need... an X-ray.   Мне (не) ну́жен... рентге́н.
Mnye (ni-) __nu__-zhîn... rin-__gyen__.

test.   ана́лиз.   *a-__na__-lis.*

shot.   уко́л.   *u-__kol__.*

768. I will (not) stay at the hospital.
Я (не) останусь в больнице.
Ya (ni-) as-<u>ta</u>-nus' vbal'-<u>ni</u>-tse.

769. How much will it cost?   Сколько это будет стоить?
<u>Skol</u>'-ka <u>e</u>-ta <u>bu</u>-dit <u>sto</u>-it'?

770. I don't have insurance.   У меня нет страховки.
U-mi-<u>nya</u> nyet stra-<u>hof</u>-ki.

771. I have insurance.   У меня есть страховка.
U-mi-<u>nya</u> yest' stra-<u>hof</u>-ka.

772. I need a receipt for my insurance company.
Мне нужна квитанция для страховки.
Mnye nuzh-<u>na</u> kvi-<u>tan</u>-tsî-ya dlya stra-<u>hof</u>-ki.

TRAVELERS WITH DISABILITIES

773. He / she is… blind. *(m./f.)*   Он / она… слепой / слепая.
On a-<u>na</u>… sli-<u>poy</u> sli-<u>pa</u>-ya.

deaf. *(m./f.)*   глухой. (хая)   *glu-<u>hoy</u>. (<u>ha</u>-ya)*

mute. *(m./f.)*   немой. (мая)   *ni-<u>moy</u>. (<u>ma</u>-ya)*

774. He / she is… autistic.   У него / неё аутизм.
U-ni-<u>vo</u> / ni-yo a-u-<u>tizm</u>.

developmentally challenged.   отсталость.   *at-<u>sta</u>-last'.*

775. I can't walk on my own.   Я не могу сам ходить.
Ya ni-ma-<u>gu</u> sam ha-<u>dit</u>'.

776. I need a wheelchair.   Мне нужна инвалидная коляска.
Mnye nuzh-<u>na</u> in-va-<u>lid</u>-na-ya ka-<u>lyas</u>-ka.

777. Is there an elevator or ramp here?
Здесь есть лифт или рампа?
Zdyes' yest' lift <u>i</u>-li <u>ram</u>-pa?

778. This is a guide dog.   Это собака-поводырь.
<u>E</u>-ta sa-<u>ba</u>-ka pa-va-<u>dîr</u>'.

779. Can I come in with the dog?   Можно войти с собакой?
<u>Mozh</u>-na vay-<u>ti</u> ssa-<u>ba</u>-kay?

EMERGENCY SITUATIONS

780. Help!   Помогите!   *Pa-ma-gi-tye!*

781. Stop!   Стой!   ***Stoy!***

782. Thief!   Вор!   ***Vor!***

783. Police!   Полиция!   *Pa-li-tsî-ya!*

784. I've been… robbed.   Меня… обокрали.
Mi-nya… a-ba-kra-li.

   beaten.   избили.   *iz-bi-li.*

   raped.   изнасиловали.   *iz-na-si-la-va-li.*

785. Fire!   Пожар!   *Pa-zhar!*

786. Call… the police.   Позовите… полицию.
Pa-za-vi-tye… pa-li-tsî-yu.

   a fire brigade.   пожарную.   *pa-zhar-nu-yu.*

   an ambulance.   скорую.   *sko-ru-yu.*

787. Where is a… police precinct?
Где… полицейский участок?
Gdye… pa-li-tsey-skiy u-chas-tak?

   hospital.   больница.   *bal'-ni-tsa.*

788. My… money has been stolen.   У меня украли… деньги.
U-mi-nya u-kra-li… dyen'-gi.

   documents.   документы.   *da-ku-myen-tî.*

   purse.   сумку.   *sum-ku.*

   wallet.   бумажник.   *bu-mazh-nik.*

789. I apologize.   Прошу прощения.
Pra-shu pra-schye-nya.

790. How much will it be?   Сколько это будет стоить?
Skol'-ka e-ta bu-dit sto-it'?

791. I'm innocent.   Я ни в чём не виноват.
Ya nif-<u>chom</u> ni-vi-na-<u>vat</u>.

792. I don't know anything.   Я ничего не знаю.
Ya ni-chi-<u>vo</u> ni-<u>zna</u>-yu.

793. I didn't… see / hear anything.
Я ничего… не видел / не слышал.
Ya ni-chi-<u>vo</u>… ni-<u>vi</u>-dil / ni-<u>sli</u>-shal.

794. I have no… weapons.   У меня нет… оружия.
U-mi-<u>nya</u> nyet… a-<u>ru</u>-zhî-ya.

    drugs.   наркотиков.   *nar-<u>ko</u>-ti-kaf.*

795. I need a… lawyer / translator.
Мне нужен… адвокат / переводчик.
Mnye <u>nu</u>-zhîn… a-dva-<u>kat</u> / pi-ri-<u>vot</u>-chik.

796. I need to call… a lawyer.
Мне нужно позвонить… адвокату.
Mnye <u>nuzh</u>-na paz-va-<u>nit</u>'… a-dva-<u>ka</u>-tu.

    the consulate.   в посольство.   *fpa-<u>sol</u>'-stva.*

Specialized Vocabulary

COMMON OCCUPATIONS

actor	актёр	*ak-tyor*
architect	архитéктор	*ar-hi-tyekt-ar*
athlete	спортсмéн	*sports-myen*
businessman / woman	бизнесмéн *(m./f.)*	*biz-nis-myen*
carpenter	плóтник	*plot-nik*
chef	пóвар	*po-var*
cleric	свящéнник	*svi-schen-nik*
computer programmer	программи́ст	*pra-gra-mist*
dentist	зубнóй врач	*zub-noy vrach*
designer	дизáйнер	*di-zay-nir*
diplomat	дипломáт	*di-pla-mat*
doctor	врач	*vrach*

driver (bus / taxi)   водńтель (автóбуса / такси́)
va-di-til' (af-to-bu-sa / tak-si)

economist	эконими́ст	*e-ka-na-mist*
engineer	инженéр	*in-zhî-nyer*
factory worker	рабóчий	*ra-bo-chiy*
farmer	фéрмер	*fyer-mir*
film director	режиссёр	*ri-zhî-syor*

flight attendant *(m./f.)*   стю́ард / стюардéсса
stu-art / stu-ar-des-sa

hairdresser	парикмáхер	*pa-rik-ma-hir*

journalist	журналист	*zhur-na-list*
judge	судья	*su-dya*
lawyer	адвкоат	*a-dva-kat*
librarian	библиотекарь	*bi-bli-a-tye-kar'*
musician	музыкант	*mu-zî-kant*
nurse	медсестра	*mid-sist-ra*
painter	художник	*hu-dozh-nik*
photographer	фотограф	*fa-to-graf*
pilot	лётчик	*lyot-chik*
police officer	полицейский	*pa-li-tsey-skiy*
professor	профессор	*pra-fye-sar*
receptionist / secretary	секретарь	*sik-ri-tar'*
salesperson	продавец	*pra-da-vyets*
scientist	учёный	*u-cho-nîy*
surgeon	хирург	*hi-rurk*
tailor	портной	*part-noy*
teacher	учитель	*u-chi-til'*
veterinarian	ветеринар	*vi-ti-ri-nar*
waiter	официант	*a-fi-tsî-ant*
writer	писатель	*pi-sa-til'*

CARDINAL NUMBERS

one	один *(m.)* / одна *(f.)* / одно *(n.)*	
	a-din / ad-na / ad-no	
two	два *(m.)* / две *(f.)*	*dva / dvye*
three	три	*tri*
four	четыре	*chi-tî-rye*
five	пять	*pyat'*
six	шесть	*shest'*
seven	семь	*sem'*

eight	во́семь	<u>_vo_</u>-sim
nine	де́вять	<u>_dye_</u>-vit'
ten	де́сять	<u>_dye_</u>-sit'
eleven	оди́ннадцать	a-<u>_di_</u>-na-tsat'
twelve	двена́дцать	dvi-<u>_na_</u>-tsat'
thirteen	трина́дцать	tri-<u>_na_</u>-tsat'
fourteen	четы́рнадцать	chi-<u>_tîr_</u>-na-tsat'
fifteen	пятна́дцать	pit-<u>_na_</u>-tsat'
sixteen	шестна́дцать	shîs-<u>_na_</u>-tsat'
seventeen	семна́дцать	sim-<u>_na_</u>-tsat'
eighteen	восемна́дцать	va-<u>_sim_</u>-na-tsat'
nineteen	девятна́дцать	di-vit-<u>_na_</u>-tsat'
twenty	два́дцать	<u>_dva_</u>-tsat'
twenty-one	два́дцать оди́н	<u>_dva_</u>-tsat' a-<u>_din_</u>
thirty	три́дцать	<u>_tri_</u>-tsat'
forty	со́рок	<u>_so_</u>-rak
fifty	пятьдеся́т	pi-di-<u>_syat_</u>
sixty	шестьдеся́т	shîz-di-<u>_syat_</u>
seventy	се́мьдесят	<u>_syem'_</u>-di-sit
eighty	во́семьдесят	<u>_vo_</u>-sim-di-sit
ninety	девяно́сто	di-vi-<u>_no_</u>-sta
one hundred	сто	sto
two hundred	две́сти	<u>_dvyes_</u>-ti
three hundred	три́ста	<u>_tris_</u>-ta
four hundred	четы́реста	chi-<u>_tî_</u>-ris-ta
five hundred	пятьсо́т	pit-<u>_sot_</u>
six hundred	шестьсо́т	shîs-<u>_sot_</u>
seven hundred	семьсо́т	sim-<u>_sot_</u>
eight hundred	восемьсо́т	va-sim-<u>_sot_</u>
nine hundred	девятьсо́т	di-vit-<u>_sot_</u>
one thousand	ты́сяча	<u>_tî_</u>-si-cha

two thousand	две ты́сячи	*dvye <u>tî</u>-si-chi*
five thousand	пять ты́сяч	*pyat' <u>tî</u>-sich*
one hundred thousand	сто ты́сячь	*sto <u>tî</u>-sich*
one million	миллио́н	*mi-li-<u>on</u>*

ORDINAL NUMBERS

first	пе́рвый (вая, вое, вые)	
	<u>pyer</u>-vîy (va-ya, va-ye, vî-ye)	
second	второ́й (ра́я, ро́е, рые)	
	fta-<u>roy</u> (<u>ra</u>-ya, <u>ro</u>-ye, <u>rî</u>-ye)	
third	тре́тий	*<u>trye</u>-tiy*
fourth	четвёртый	*chit-<u>vyor</u>-tiy*
fifth	пя́тый	*<u>pya</u>-tiy*
sixth	шесто́й	*shîs-<u>toy</u>*
seventh	седьмо́й	*sid'-<u>moy</u>*
eighth	восьмо́й	*vas'-<u>moy</u>*
ninth	девя́тый	*di-<u>vya</u>-tiy*
tenth	деся́тый	*di-<u>sya</u>-tiy*
eleventh	оди́ннадцатый	*a-<u>di</u>-na-tsa-tîy*
twelfth	двена́дцатый	*dvi-<u>na</u>-tsa-tîy*
thirteenth	трина́дцатый	*tri-<u>na</u>-tsa-tîy*
fourteenth	четы́рнадцатый	*chi-<u>tîr</u>-na-tsa-tîy*
fifteenth	пятна́дцатый	*pit-<u>na</u>-tsa-tîy*
sixteenth	шестна́дцатый	*shîs-<u>na</u>-tsa-tîy*
seventeenth	семна́дцатый	*sim-<u>na</u>-tsa-tîy*
eighteenth	восемна́дцатый	*va-sim-<u>na</u>-tsa-tîy*
nineteenth	девятна́дцатый	*di-vit-<u>na</u>-tsa-tîy*
twentieth	двадца́тый	*dva-<u>tsa</u>-tîy*
thirtieth	тридца́тый	*tri-<u>tsa</u>-tîy*
fortieth	сороково́й	*sa-ra-ka-<u>voy</u>*

fiftieth	пятидеся́тый	*pi-ti-di-<u>sya</u>-tîy*
sixtieth	шестидеся́тый	*shîs-ti-di-<u>sya</u>-tîy*
seventieth	семидеся́тый	*si-mi-di-<u>sya</u>-tîy*
eightieth	восьмидеся́тый	*vas'-mi-di-<u>sya</u>-tîy*
ninetieth	девяно́стый	*di-vi-<u>nos</u>-tîy*
one hundredth	со́тый	*<u>so</u>-tîy*

DAYS OF THE WEEK

Monday	понеде́льник	*pa-ni-<u>dyel</u>'-nik*
Tuesday	вто́рник	*<u>ftor</u>-nik*
Wednesday	среда́	*sri-<u>da</u>*
Thursday	четве́рг	*chit-<u>vyerk</u>*
Friday	пя́тница	*<u>pyat</u>-ni-tsa*
Saturday	суббо́та	*su-<u>bo</u>-ta*
Sunday	воскресе́нье	*vas-kri-<u>syen</u>-ye*

MONTHS

January	янва́рь	*yin-<u>var</u>'*
February	февра́ль	*fiv-<u>ral</u>'*
March	март	*mart*
April	апре́ль	*a-<u>pryel</u>'*
May	май	*may*
June	ию́нь	*i-<u>yun</u>'*
July	ию́ль	*i-<u>yul</u>'*
August	а́вгуст	*<u>av</u>-gust*
September	сентя́брь	*sin-<u>tyabr</u>'*
October	октя́брь	*ak-<u>tyabr</u>'*
November	ноя́брь	*na-<u>yabr</u>'*
December	дека́брь	*di-<u>kabr</u>'*

NATIONAL HOLIDAYS

New Year's Day
  January 1   пе́рвое января́   ***pyer*-va-ye yin-va-*rya***

Orthodox Christmas
  January 7   седьмо́е января́   ***sid'-mo*-ye yin-va-*rya***

Day of the Defender of the Fatherland
  February 23   два́дцать тре́тье февраля́
  dva*-tsat' *trye*-tye fiv-ra-*lya

International Women's Day
  March 8   восьмо́е ма́рта   ***vas'-mo*-ye *mar*-ta**

Easter
  April 15   пятна́дцатое апре́ля
  ***pit-na*-tsa-ta-ye a-*prye*-lya**

Day of Spring and Labor
  May 1   пе́рвое ма́я   ***pyer*-va-ye *ma*-ya**

Victory Day
  May 9   девя́тое ма́я   ***di-vya*-ta-ye *ma*-ya**

Russia Day
  June 12   двенадца́тое ию́ня   ***dvi-na*-tsa-ta-ye i-*yu*-nya**

Day of National Unity
  November 4   четвёртое ноября́
  chi-tvyor*-ta-ye na-ib-*rya

VEGETABLES

asparagus   спа́ржа   ***spar*-zha**
beans   фасо́ль   ***fa-sol'***
beets   свёкла   ***svyo*-kla**
broccoli   бро́кколи   ***bro*-ka-li**

brussels sprouts	брюссéльская капýста	
	bryu-sel'-ska-ya ka-pus-ta	
cabbage	капýста	*ka-pus-ta*
carrots	морквь	*mar-kof'*
cauliflower	цветнáя капуста	*tsvit-na-ya ka-pus-ta*
celery	сельдерéй	*sil'-di-ryei*
corn (maize)	кукурýза	*ku-ku-ru-za*
cucumber	огурéц	*a-gu-ryets*
eggplant	баклажáн	*ba-kla-zhan*
garlic	чеснк	*chis-nok*
green onion	зелёный лук	*zi-lyo-niy luk*
lettuce	салáт	*sa-lat*
onion	лук	*luk*
parsley	петрýшка	*pi-trush-ka*
peas	горх	*ga-rokh*
pepper	пéрец	*pye-rits*
pickles	солёные огурцы́	*sa-lyo-nî-ye a-gur-tsî*
potatoes	кртшка	*kar-tosh-ka*
spinach	шпинáт	*shpi-nat*
tomato	помидр	*pa-mi-dor*

FRUITS

apples	яблоки	*ya-bla-ki*
apricots	абриксы	*a-bri-ko-sî*
bananas	банáны	*ba-na-nî*
blueberry	черника	*chir-ni-ka*
cherry	черéшня	*chi-ryesh-nya*
dates	фники	*fi-ni-ki*
grapefruit	грейпфрýт	*greyp-frut*
grapes	виногрáд	*vi-na-grat*

lemons	лимо́ны	*li-**mo**-nî*
mandarins	мандари́ны	*man-da-**ri**-nî*
mango	ма́нго	***man**-go*
olives	оли́вки	*a-**lif**-ki*
oranges	апельси́ны	*a-pil'-**si**-nî*
peaches	пе́рсики	***pyer**-si-ki*
pears	гру́ши	***gru**-shî*
pineapple	анана́с	*a-na-**nas***
plums	сли́вы	***sli**-vî*
raspberry	мали́на	*ma-**li**-na*
strawberry	клубни́ка	*klub-**ni**-ka*
watermelon	арбу́з	*ar-**bus***

MEAT PRODUCTS

beef	говя́дина	*ga-**vya**-di-na*
chicken	ку́рица	***ku**-ri-tsa*
ham	ветчина́	*vit-chi-na*
lamb	бара́нина	*ba-**ra**-ni-na*
pork	свини́на	*svi-**ni**-na*
salami	колбаса́	*kal-ba-**sa***
sausages	соси́ски	*sa-**sis**-ki*
turkey	инде́йка	*in-**dey**-ka*
veal	теля́тина	*ti-**lya**-ti-na*

FISH

bass	о́кунь	***o**-kun'*
carp	карп	*karp*
catfish	сом	*som*
clams	клэм	*klem*

cod	треска́	*tris-ka*
eel	у́горь	*u-gar'*
flounder	камбала́	*kam-ba-la*
halibut	па́лтус	*pal-tus*
herring	селёдка	*si-lyot-ka*
lobster	рак	*rak*
mussels	ми́дии	*mi-di-i*
oysters	у́стрицы	*us-tri-tsî*
pike	щу́ка	*schu-ka*
salmon	лосо́сь	*la-sos'*
sardines	сарди́ны	*sar-di-nî*
scallops	гребешки́	*gri-bish-ki*
shrimp	креве́тки	*kri-vyet-ki*
snapper	снэ́ппер	*sne-pir*
sturgeon	осётр	*a-syotr*
swordfish	меч-ры́ба	*myech-rî-ba*
tilapia	тиля́пия	*ti-lya-pi-ya*
trout	форе́ль	*fa-ryel'*
tuna	туне́ц	*tu-nyets*

ALCOHOLIC DRINKS

beer	пи́во	*pi-va*
cognac	конья́к	*kan-yak*
liquor	ликёр	*li-kyor*
scotch	скотч	*skotch*
vodka	во́дка	*vot-ka*
whiskey	ви́ски	*vis-ki*
wine (red)	кра́сное вино́	*kras-na-ye vi-no*
wine (white)	бе́лое вино́	*bye-la-ye vi-no*

BREAD

baguette	батóн	***ba-<u>ton</u>***
cake	торт	***tort***
cookie(s)	печéнье	***pi-<u>chyen</u>'-ye***
croissant	рожóк	***ra-<u>zhok</u>***
pastry	пирóжное	***pi-<u>rozh</u>-na-ye***
pie	пирóг	***pi-<u>rok</u>***
rye bread	чёрный хлеб	***<u>chor</u>-niy hlyep***
white bread	бýлка	***<u>bul</u>-ka***

DAIRY PRODUCTS

baked yogurt	ря́женка	***<u>rya</u>-zhin-ka***
butter	мáсло сли́вочное	***<u>mas</u>-la <u>sli</u>-vach-na-ye***
cheese	сыр	***sîr***
cream	сли́вки	***<u>slif</u>-ki***
farmers cheese	творóг	***tva-<u>rok</u>***
feta	бры́нза	***<u>brîn</u>-za***
kefir	кефи́р	***ki-<u>fir</u>***
milk	молокó	***ma-la-<u>ko</u>***
yogurt	йóгурт	***<u>yo</u>-gurt***
sour cream	сметáна	***smi-<u>ta</u>-na***

OTHER FOOD ITEMS

buckwheat	грéчневая кáша	***<u>gryech</u>-ni-va-ya <u>ka</u>-sha***
candy	конфéты	***kan-<u>fye</u>-tî***
chocolate	шоколáд	***sho-ka-<u>lat</u>***
coffee	кóфе	***<u>ko</u>-fye***
dried fruit	сухофрýкты	***su-ha-<u>fruk</u>-tî***

eggs	я́йца	*yay-tsa*
flour	мука́	*mu-ka*
jam	варе́нье	*va-ryen'-ye*
nuts	оре́хи	*a-rye-hi*
olive oil	ма́сло оли́вковое	*mas-la a-lif-ka-va-ye*
pasta (macaroni)	макаро́ны	*ma-ka-ro-nî*
rice	рис	*ris*
salt	соль	*sol'*
sauce	со́ус	*so-us*
spices	спе́ции	*spye-tsî-i*
sugar	са́хар	*sa-har*
tea	чай	*chay*

MEALS AND COURSES

breakfast	за́втрак	*zaf-trak*
lunch	ланч, второ́й за́втрак	*lanch, fta-roy zaf-trak*
dinner	обе́д	*a-byet*
supper	у́жин	*u-zhîn*
first course	пе́рвое	*pyer-va-ye*
second course	второ́е	*fta-ro-ye*
appetizer	заку́ска	*za-kus-ka*
dessert	десе́рт	*di-syert*

TABLEWARE

bottle	буты́лка	*bu-tîl-ka*
bowl	ми́ска	*mis-ka*
carafe	графи́н	*gra-fin*
cup	ча́шка	*chash-ka*
dish	блю́до	*blyu-da*

fork	ви́лка	*vil-ka*
glass	стака́н	*sta-kan*
knife	нож	*nosh*
napkin	салфе́тка	*sal-fyet-ka*
pepper-mill	пе́речница	*pye-rich-ni-tsa*
plate	таре́лка	*ta-ryel-ka*
salt shaker	соло́нка	*sa-lon-ka*
spoon	ло́жка	*losh-ka*
tablecloth	ска́терть	*ska-tirt'*
teaspoon	ча́йная ло́жка	*chay-na-ya losh-ka*
wine glass	рю́мка	*ryum-ka*

SOUPS

borsch	борщ	*borsch*
bullion	бульо́н	*bul'-yon*
cabbage soup	щи	*schi*
chorba	шурпа́	*shur-pa*
fish soup	уха́	*u-ha*
French onion soup	францу́зский лу́ковый суп	
fran-tsus-kiy lu-ka-viy sup		
fruit soup	фрукто́вый суп	*fruk-to-viy sup*
pea soup	горо́ховый суп	*ga-ro-ha-viy sup*
tomato soup	тома́тный суп	*ta-mat-niy sup*
vegetable soup	овощно́й суп	*a-vasch-noy sup*

MEAT DISHES

aspic	сту́день	*stu-din'*
bacon	са́ло	*sa-la*
cutlet	котле́та	*kat-lye-ta*

fat жир *zhîr*

ham ветчина́ *vit-chi-na*

kidneys по́чки *poch-ki*

liver печёнка *pi-chon-ka*

ribs рёбрышки *ryob-rîsh-ki*

salami колбаса́ *kal-ba-sa*

sausage соси́ски *sa-sis-ki*

schnitzel шни́цель *shni-tsîl'*

steak бифште́кс *bif-shteks*

stew жарко́е *zhar-ko-ye*

tongue язы́к *yi-zîk*

OTHER DISHES

crêpes бли́нчики *blin-chi-ki*

sandwich with... бутербро́д с... *bu-ter-brot s...*

"gnocchi" варе́ники *va-rye-ni-ki*

boiled potatoes варёный карто́фель
va-ryo-nîy kar-to-fil'

stuffed cabbage голубцы́ *ga-lup-tsî*

mushrooms грибы́ *gri-bî*

fried potatoes жа́реный карто́фель *zha-ri-nîy kar-to-fil'*

compote компо́т *kam-pot*

pasta лапша́ *lap-sha*

dumplings пельме́ни *pil'-mye-ni*

stuffed buns пирожки́ *pi-rash-ki*

mashed potatoes пюре́ *pyu-re*

crayfish ра́ки *ra-ki*

rice рис *ris*

salad сала́т *sa-lat*

SPICES AND CONDIMENTS

mustard	горчи́ца	*gar-**chi**-tsa*
ketchup	ке́тчуп	***ket**-chup*
cinnamon	кори́ца	*ka-**ri**-tsa*
red pepper	кра́сный пе́рец	***kras**-niy **pye**-rits*
bay leaf	лавро́вый лист	*lav-**ro**-viy list*
lemon	лимо́н	*li-**mon***
hot sauce	о́стрый со́ус	***ost**-riy **so**-us*
salt	соль	*sol'*
dill	укро́п	*u-**krop***
vinegar	у́ксус	***uk**-sus*

FLAVORS

bitter	го́рький	***gor**'-kiy*
salty	солёный	*sa-**lyo**-niy*
sour	ки́слый	***kis**-liy*
spicy	о́стрый	***ost**-riy*
sweet	сла́дкий	***slat**-kiy*

ACCESSORIES

belt	по́яс	***po**-is*
bracelet	брасле́т	*bra-**slyet***
cufflinks	за́понки	***za**-pan-ki*
earrings	се́рьги	***syer**'-gi*
gloves	перча́тки	*pir-**chat**-ki*
handkerchief	носово́й плато́к	*na-sa-**voy** pla-**tok***
necklace	ожере́лье	*a-zhî-**ryel**'-ye*
purse	су́мочка	***su**-mach-ka*

scarf	шарф	*sharf*
stockings	чулки́	*chul-**ki***
sunglasses	очки́отсо́лнца	*ach-**ki** at-**son**-tsa*
umbrella	зо́нтик	***zon**-tik*
watch	часы́	*cha-**sî***
woman's hat	шля́пка	***shlyap**-ka*

SHAPE, FORM, SIZE, QUALITY

big	большо́й (ша́я, шо́е, ши́е)	
	*bal'-**shoy** (-**sha**-ya, -**sho**-ye, -**shî**-ye)*	
small	ма́ленький (кая, кое, кие)	
	ma-lin'-kiy (-ka-ya, -ko-ye, -ki-ye)	
tall / high	высо́кий	*vî-**so**-kiy*
short / low	ни́зкий	***nis**-kiy*
wide	широ́кий	*shî-**ro**-kiy*
narrow	у́зкий	***us**-kiy*
deep	глубо́кий	*glu-**bo**-kiy*
shallow	ме́лкий	***myel**-kiy*
thick / fat	то́лстый	***tol**-stîy*
thin / skinny	то́нкий	***ton**-kiy*
round	кру́глый	***kru**-glîy*
square	квадра́тный	*kvad-**rat**-nîy*
rectangular	прямоуго́льный	*prya-ma-u-**gol'**-nîy*
curved / crooked	криво́й	*kri-**voy***
flat	пло́ский	***plos**-kiy*
full	по́лный	***pol**-nîy*
empty	пусто́й	*pus-**toy***
dry	сухо́й	*su-**hoy***
moist	вла́жный	***vlazh**-nîy*
wet	мо́крый	***mo**-krîy*

hot	горя́чий	*ga-rya-chiy*
warm	тёплый	*tyop-liy*
cold	холо́дный	*ha-lod-niy*
hard	твёрдый	*tvyor-diy*
soft	мя́гкий	*myah-kiy*
sharp	о́стрый	*ost-riy*
dull	тупо́й	*tu-poy*
rough	шерша́вый	*shir-sha-viy*
smooth	гла́дкий	*glat-kiy*
beautiful	краси́вый	*kra-si-viy*
ugly	уро́дливый	*u-rod-li-viy*
average	сре́дний	*sryed-niy*

COLORS

black	чёрный (ная, ное, ные)	
chor-niy (-na-ya, no-ye, nî-ye)		
white	бе́лый (лая, лое, лые)	*bye-liy (-la-ya, lo-ye, lî-ye)*
brown	кори́чневый	*ka-rich-ni-viy*
red	кра́сный	*kras-niy*
pink	ро́зовый	*ro-za-viy*
orange	ора́нжевый	*a-ran-zhî-viy*
yellow	жёлтый	*zhol-tiy*
green	зелёный	*zi-lyo-niy*
light blue	голубо́й	*ga-lu-boy*
dark blue	си́ний	*si-niy*
violet	фиоле́товый	*fi-a-lye-ta-viy*
light-	све́тло-	*svyet-la-*
dark-	тёмно-	*tyom-na-*

PERSONAL CARE ITEMS

conditioner	кондиционéр	*kan-di-tsî-a-<u>nyer</u>*
dental floss	флосс	*flos*
deodorant	дезодорáнт	*di-za-da-<u>rant</u>*
mouthwash	полоскáние для рта	
pa-las-<u>ka</u>-ni-ye dlya <u>rta</u>		
nail clippers	щúпчики (для ногтéй)	
<u>schip</u>-chi-ki (dlya nah-<u>tey</u>)		
razors	брúтвы	*<u>brit</u>-vî*
shampoo	шампýнь	*sham-<u>pun</u>'*
shaving cream	крем для бритья́	*kryem dlya bri-<u>tya</u>*
soap	мы́ло	*<u>mi</u>-la*
sunblock	крем от сóлнца	*kryem at <u>son</u>-tsa*
tanning cream	крем для загáра	*kryem dlya za-<u>ga</u>-ra*
toilet paper	туалéтная бумáга	*tu-a-<u>lyet</u>-na-ya bu-<u>ma</u>-ga*
toothbrush	зубнáя щётка	*zub-<u>na</u>-ya <u>schot</u>-ka*
toothpaste	зубнáя пáста	*zub-<u>na</u>-ya <u>pas</u>-ta*

COSMETICS

cologne	одеколóн	*a-de-ka-<u>lon</u>*
foundation cream	крем-оснóва	*kryem as-<u>no</u>-va*
lipstick	помáда	*pa-<u>ma</u>-da*
mascara	тушь для реснúц	*tush dlya ris-<u>nits</u>*
nail polish	лак для ногтéй	*lak dlya nah-<u>tey</u>*
perfume	духú	*du-<u>hi</u>*
powder	пýдра	*<u>pu</u>-dra*
rouge	румя́на	*ru-<u>mya</u>-na*
skin toner	тóник для кóжи	*<u>to</u>-nik dlya <u>ko</u>-zhî*

CULTURAL AND PERFORMING ARTS

act	акт	*akt*
actor	актёр	*ak-tyor*
actress	актри́са	*ak-tri-sa*
applause	аплодисме́нты	*a-pla-dis-myen-tî*
balcony	балко́н	*bal-kon*
ballerina	балери́на	*ba-li-ri-na*
ballet	бале́т	*ba-lyet*
box	ло́жа	*lo-zha*
cinema	кинотеа́тр	*ki-na-ti-atr*
coat check	гардеро́б	*gar-di-rop*
comedy	коме́дия	*ka-mye-di-ya*
concert	конце́рт	*kan-tsert*
conductor	дирижёр	*di-ri-zhor*
dancer	танцо́вщик	*tan-tsof-schik*
drama	дра́ма	*dra-ma*
film	фильм	*fil'm*
grand piano	роя́ль	*ro-yal'*
instrument	инструме́нт	*in-stru-myent*
intermission	антра́кт	*an-trakt*
music	му́зыка	*mu-zî-ka*
chamber	ка́мерная	*ka-mir-na-ya*
classical	класси́ческая	*kla-si-chis-ka-ya*
folk	наро́дная	*na-rod-na-ya*
opera	о́пера	*o-pi-ra*
orchestra	орке́стр	*ar-kyestr*
parterre	парте́р	*par-ter*
play	спекта́кль	*spik-takl'*
poster	афи́ша	*a-fi-sha*

program	прогрáмма	*pro-gra-ma*
role	роль	*rol'*
screen	экрáн	*ek-ran*
seat	мéсто	*myes-ta*
singer	певéц	*pi-vyets*

SPORTS

archery	стрельбá из лýка	*stril'-ba iz-lu-ka*
badminton	бадминтóн	*bad-min-ton*
baseball	бейсбóл	*byeys-bol*
basketball	баскетбóл	*bas-kid-bol*
bobsled	бобслéй	*bap-slyey*
bowling	бóулинг	*bou-link*
boxing	бокс	*boks*
croquet	крокéт	*kra-ket*
fencing	фехтовáние	*fih-ta-va-ni-ye*
figure skating	фигýрное катáние	

fi-gur-na-ye ka-ta-ni-ye

golf	гольф	*gol'f*
gymnastics	гимнáстика	*gim-nas-ti-ka*
handball	гандбóл	*gand-bol*
high jump	прыжкú в высотý	*prîsh-ki vvî-sa-tu*
hockey	хоккéй	*ha-kyey*
judo	дзюдó	*dzyu-do*
karate	каратэ́	*ka-ra-te*
lacrosse	лакрóсс	*la-kros*
long jump	прыжкú в длинý	*prîsh-ki vdli-nu*
mountain climbing	скалолáзанье	*ska-la-la-zan'-ye*
ping-pong	пинг-пóнг	*pin-ponk*
rowing	грéбля	*gryeb-lya*

skateboarding	скейтбо́рдинг	*skeyt-<u>bor</u>-dink*
skiing	лы́жи	*<u>li</u>-zhî*
snowboarding	сноубо́рдинг	*sno-u-<u>bor</u>-dink*
soccer	футбо́л	*fud-<u>bol</u>*
sumo wrestling	борьба́ су́мо	*bor'-<u>ba</u> <u>su</u>-mo*
surfing	сёрфинг	*<u>syor</u>-fink*
swimming	пла́вание	*<u>pla</u>-va-nye*
tennis	те́ннис	*<u>te</u>-nis*
volleyball	волейбо́л	*va-liy-<u>bol</u>*
water polo	ватерпо́ло	*va-ter-<u>po</u>-lo*
waterskiing	во́дные лы́жи	*<u>vod</u>-nî-ye <u>li</u>-zhî*
yoga	йо́га	*<u>yo</u>-ga*

PARTS OF THE BODY

backside	зад	*zat*
blood	кровь	*krof'*
bone	кость	*kost'*
breasts	гру́ди	*<u>gru</u>-di*
cheek	щека́	*schi-<u>ka</u>*
chest	грудь	*grut'*
chin	подборо́док	*pad-ba-<u>ro</u>-dak*
ear	у́хо / у́ши (*sing./pl.*)	*<u>u</u>-ho / <u>u</u>-shî*
elbow	ло́коть / ло́кти (*sing./pl.*)	*<u>lo</u>-kat' / <u>lok</u>-ti*
eye	глаз / глаза́ (*sing./pl.*)	*glas / gla-<u>za</u>*
face	лицо́	*li-<u>tso</u>*
finger	па́лец / па́льцы (*sing./pl.*)	*<u>pa</u>-lits / <u>pal</u>'-tsî*
forehead	лоб	*lop*
hair	во́лосы	*<u>vo</u>-la-sî*
hand	рука́ / ру́ки (*sing./pl.*)	*ru-<u>ka</u> / <u>ru</u>-ki*
head	голова́	*ga-la-<u>va</u>*

heart	сéрдце	_syer-tse_
heel	пя́тка / пя́тки (*sing./pl.*)	_pyat-ka / pyat-ki_
hip	бедрó	_bid-ro_
jaw	чéлюсть	_che-lyust'_
joint	сустáв / сустáвы (*sing./pl.*)	_sus-taf / sus-ta-vî_
kidney	пóчка / пóчки (*sing./pl.*)	_poch-ka / poch-ki_
knee	колéно / колéни (*sing./pl.*)	_ka-lye-na / ka-lye-ni_
leg / foot	ногá / нóги (*sing./pl.*)	_no-ga / no-gi_
lip	губá / гу́бы(*sing./pl.*)	_gu-ba / gu-bî_
liver	пéчень	_pye-chin'_
lungs	лёгкие	_lyoh-ki-ye_
mouth	рот	_rot_
muscle	мы́шца / мы́шцы (*sing./pl.*)	_mîsh-tsa / mîsh-tsî_
neck	шéя	_she-ya_
nerve	нерв	_nyerf_
nipple	сосóк / соски́ (*sing./pl.*)	_sa-sok / sas-ki_
nose	нос	_nos_
palm	ладóнь / ладóни (*sing./pl.*)	_la-don' / la-do-ni_
pelvis	таз	_tas_
rib	ребро / рёбра (*sing./pl.*)	_rib-ro / ryob-ra_
sexual organs	половы́еóрганы	_pa-la-vî-ye or-ga-nî_
shoulder	плечó / плéчи (*sing./pl.*)	_plye-cho / plye-chi_
skin	кóжа	_ko-zha_
sole	ступня́ / сту́пни (*sing./pl.*)	_stup-nya / stup-ni_
spine	позвонóчник	_pa-zva-noch-nik_

Index

Numbers refer to entry numbers.